The Great Escape

It is the Second World War. A group of British prisoners, shot down over Germany, are trapped in a prison camp. Snow hangs on the ugly barbed-wire all around them and German guards with machine-guns stamp their feet in the cold.

Roger Bushell, a young squadron leader, has an amazing plan. Days and months of back-breaking work could mean freedom for 220 men.

But all the time the Germans plan spot-checks to stop any escapes. Search-lights sweep over the camp every night and no one really knows the price they may have to pay if they are found out.

D0420588

The BULLS-EYE series
General Editor   PATRICK NOBES

The Great Escape

Adapted by Sue Gee
from *The Great Escape*
by Paul Brickhill

Hutchinson

London Melbourne Sydney Auckland Johannesburg

Hutchinson Education

An imprint of Century Hutchinson Ltd
62−65 Chandos Place, London WC2N 4NW

Century Hutchinson Australia Pty Ltd
16−22 Church Street, Hawthorn, Melbourne, Victoria 3122, Australia

Century Hutchinson New Zealand Ltd
PO Box 40 − 086, Glenfield, Auckland 10, New Zealand

Century Hutchinson South Africa (Pty) Ltd
PO Box 337, Bergvlei 2012, South Africa

First published by Faber and Faber Ltd 1951
© Paul Brickhill 1951

This adaptation first published 1981
© Sue Gee 1981
Reprinted 1982 (twice), 1985, 1987

Set in VIP Baskerville by
A-Line Services, Saffron Walden, Essex

Printed and bound in Great Britain by
Anchor Brendon Limited, Tiptree, Essex

British Library Cataloguing in Publication Data
Gee, Sue
    The great escape. − (Bulls-eye)
    1. World War, 1939 − 1945 − Prisoners and
    prisons, German − Juvenile literature
    I. Title   II. Brickhill, Paul *Great escape.*
    Adaptations
    940.54'72'430924   D805.G3

ISBN 0 09 141021 5

Contents

Figures

The camp at Sagan

Towards the end of 1942 a man called Roger Bushell arrived at a German prisoner-of-war camp. It was not the first time he had been in such a camp, but he was determined it would be the last.

Roger Bushell was 32, a brave squadron leader in the Royal Air Force. In his early twenties he had been British ski champion, and a skiing accident had left a scar on his right eye that made it droop. He was a very clever man, who had been a lawyer before the war. Roger was a born leader.

The camp he came to was called Stalag Luft III. It was a new camp, built by the Germans at Sagan, near the Polish border. This was a long way from any friendly or neutral country. The Germans had built it especially for prisoners from the RAF who has been shot down when flying over Germany.

It was a grim place. There were six low, dreary wooden huts. A barbed-wire fence almost three metres high ran all the way round. About nine metres inside the barbed-wire fence was a warning wire, 45 centimetres high. If anyone put a foot over it, he was pretty sure to be shot.

Just outside the barbed-wire were sentry-boxes, on stilts, just over four-and-a-half metres high. From these huts the German sentries could look down on the camp with search-lights. All the sentries had machine-guns.

The prisoners called the Germans 'goons', and the sentry-boxes were known as 'goon-boxes'. There were special guards, whom the prisoners called 'ferrets'. They were dressed in overalls, and they had steel spikes to dig the ground, and sound-detectors to pick up the sound of digging. This was to stop prisoners tunnelling out of the camp.

If any prisoner did anything wrong, he was put in the 'cooler'. This was the name the prisoners gave to a block of cells, where you were locked up alone.

When Roger arrived in Sagan, the Gestapo had been questioning him for many months, after his last escape from a camp called Barth, on the shores of the Baltic Sea. The Gestapo had tried to prove that Roger was a spy. But Roger was too clever for them, and they had not shot him.

By the time he got to Sagan, Roger was a changed man. He once thought that escaping was a good, risky sport, like skiing. Now he was more moody, and the gaze from his wounded eye was grim.

He had seen the Germans torture people. He had been in prison camps for almost three years, after being shot down over France. There was only one German he did not hate, and that was the Chief Censor Officer at Sagan, a man called Von Masse. This man had forced the Gestapo to release him, and send him to Sagan.

His hatred had clear aims: he wanted to escape, to get back to England, and help to win the war.

When Roger came to Sagan, he became the leader of 'X Organization'. This was a group of men with many talents. All of them had made escape attempts before. Roger was known as 'Big X'.

All these men had one thing in common. They wanted to get out of Sagan.

1 The master plan

It looked like being a long war. The Germans were building a new compound at the Sagan camp. In the pine-wood across the compound where the Germans worked and kept watch, thin Russian prisoners had cut down trees to make a clearing. Workmen were putting up new huts.

Pieber, one of the German officers, said to Roger, 'You will be happier in the new compound.' Pieber had known Roger in the camp at Barth. He was a kindly little man, with scars on his cheeks. If he had been an officer in hell and you had come in screaming he would have wished you a happy stay.

'Most of you will be going to the new compound,' he went on. 'You will have taps in your huts and even lavatories.'

He told Roger that the move would be in March. Roger looked at the snow on the ugly wire and thought about summer, the escape season.

He called some of the men together: Wally Floody, Crump, Peter Fanshawe and others. He told them that they would move to the new compound in the spring.

'We must start planning now,' he said. 'I've got an idea. I want to build three tunnels at the same time, and use about 500 men. The goons might find a couple of tunnels, but we should make it with at least one. What do you think?'

The men all agreed it was a good idea. 'Good show!' said Crump, the Scot. The meeting went on for two hours. By the end they had decided on the basic plans.

They would dig three tunnels, each nine metres deep, using underground railways and workshops. They would forge passes, alter uniforms, make compasses and maps.

They would have a huge information and security organization.

Roger took the details to Massey, the senior British officer in the camp. Massey had a wounded foot. He lay on his bunk, smoking his pipe, and listened. He thought the plans were good. But he told Roger that he must lie low for a while, and leave the work to others. Roger had been in too many escapes already.

'I don't want you to get a bullet in the back of the head,' said Massey.

'They're not going to get me this time,' said Roger.

'Well, for God's sake be careful,' said Massey. 'Keep in the background. I'll make sure that you have the whole camp behind you.' Massey knew that he couldn't escape himself. The wound in his foot meant that he could only walk with a stick.

Roger got his men together, and one by one he walked them round the circuit. The circuit was a beaten track round the compound, just inside the warning wire. You could walk and talk there for hours, and the ferrets couldn't hear what you said.

Roger told Tim Walenn, who was an expert artist, that he wanted 200 forged passes. Walenn was a very polite man. But when he heard this he swore. He said that he didn't think it was possible – every pass would have to be written by hand. Roger took no notice, and told Tim to get on with the job.

He told Tommy Guest, who was very clever with a needle and thread, that he wanted 200 outfits of civilian clothes. Guest said it was impossible. They had no materials and nowhere to hide anything. 'Make your own materials,' said Roger. 'We will think about hiding the clothes when the time comes.'

Roger told Al Hake, an Australian, to make 200 compasses. He told Des Plunkett that he wanted 2000 maps. And he told Johnny Travis, who had made the lamps and tools at another camp, about all the railways, air-pumps and pipes that would be needed. Travis was a clever man. He could make lamps from old tins, using boiled margarine for fuel, and pyjama cords for wicks. He made shovels from bits of old metal, and chisels from old table knives. But when he heard what Roger wanted him to do, he nearly had a fit.

Roger want to see Massey again. Massey arranged with the German Commander to send some prisoners over to help in the new compound. Roger, Floody, Crump and Fanshawe went with these working parties.

Inside the new compound, they mapped the layout, and took measurements. Back in their own compound, they put all this information together and worked out where to dig the tunnels and how long they must be.

Roger was in charge of each stage of the growing organization. He had a mind like a filing cabinet. Once he had given a man a job, he never interfered with him. But he was always there to listen and to help. He walked round the camp in an old RAF coat, and his twisted eye took in everything. Every day he went to Massey, and they talked over the master plan.

By the end of March, the new compound was ready. So was the 'X Organization'.

2 The move

The move was on April Fool's Day. There were 700 scruffy prisoners in a straggling line. They carried cooking pots, plates, mugs and gadgets made from old tins. Some had Red Cross cardboard boxes with a little food, photos, nails, string and other treasures. All their uniforms were ragged.

Happy cursing filled the air. The change was like a holiday.

From now on, the old home was known as east compound. The new one was north compound. The Germans searched all the prisoners as they reached the north compound, but no one had anything important taken from them. Travis brought his tools, and Tim Walenn brought his forging pens and inks. Then the prisoners were marched at gun-point into their new home.

North compound was not pretty. It was about 90 metres square, with two fences of barbed-wire all the way round, just under three metres high and one-and-a-half metres apart. The warning wire was nine metres inside this fence. Just outside the northern wire were the sick quarters and the cooler.

There were goon-boxes all round the fences. At night more sentries walked round the compound. So did a guard with a fierce Alsatian dog.

There were fifteen bare wooden huts for the prisoners, in three rows in the northern half of the compound. The rest was just loose grey dirt, to be used as an exercise yard. It was also used for roll-call: each man's name was called every morning, to make sure no had escaped.

There were woods all round the compound; not pretty green woods, but thin bare pine-trees, packed close together in the dry grey earth. The trees were everywhere you looked, and they made the prisoners feel even more cut off from the world. The Germans had cut the trees back about 27 metres. This meant that any tunnels would have to reach 30 metres beyond the wire.

The huts each had eighteen small rooms. Eight men lived in each room. There were three little rooms for two people, kept for more senior officers. The furniture in the huts was very plain: bunks, a table, stools and lockers.

The bunks were made of wooden planks. The planks for the thin mattresses were just the right size for propping up the sides of tunnels!

There was only one stove for a hundred men, but there wasn't much food to cook anyway. For breakfast, lunch and dinner there was just bread, marge and jam. Sometimes there were potatoes, and every three weeks a little horse-meat.

There was a mad rush for rooms. That first day, and the next three days, were very muddled, for the prisoners and for the Germans. The 'X Organization' made the most of the muddle. Escape-fever hit the camp.

3 'Tom', 'Dick' and 'Harry'

Roger chose a man from each hut, to be known as 'Little X'. It was the job of 'Little X' to plan all the escape-work in each hut. Roger then chose his second-in-command: Conk Canton, a man built like a pocket battleship.

Roger picked a tunnel team: Wally Floody was chief, with Crump, Johnny Marshall and Johnny Bull under him. Fanshawe was put in charge of getting rid of the sand from the digging. George Harsh, an American, was in charge of tunnel security, making sure that the diggers could not be found out.

All these men met almost every day with Roger, to make plans.

Roger decided on where the three tunnels were going to be. He called them by names: 'Tom', 'Dick' and 'Harry'.

'The tunnels are only to be called by their names,' he said. 'If any idiot uses the word "tunnel" carelessly, there'll be trouble.'

The first tunnel, 'Tom', was to go from hut 123 out under the west wire to the woods beyond. This hut was farthest from the gate: it would be quiet there, and if there was a

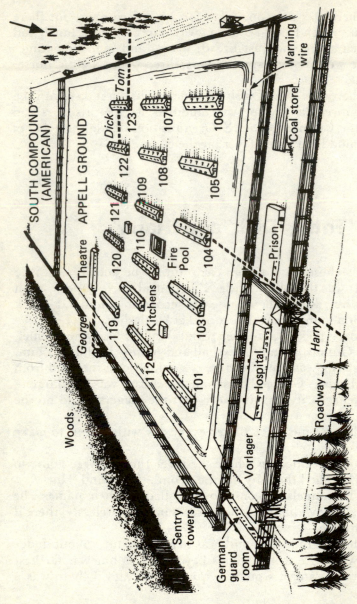

Layout of the north compound

N

SOUTH COMPOUND (AMERICAN)

APPELL GROUND

Warning wire

Coal store

Prison

Hospital

Vorlager

Roadway

Harry

Tom

Dick

George

Theatre

Kitchens

Fire Pool

Woods

Sentry towers

German guard room

101 112 119 120 121 122 123
103 110 109 108 107
104 105 106

sudden search by the Germans there would be time to warn the diggers. Of course, just because it was farthest from the gate, the Germans would have their eyes on this hut. But you can't have everything.

The second tunnel, 'Dick', was to go from hut 122, also out under the west wire. This was an inside hut, so the Germans would not have their eyes on it.

The third tunnel, 'Harry', was to go from hut 104 out under the north wire, by the gate. This meant that the diggers would have to dig an extra 30 metres, under the second wire. But it meant that the Germans would not expect a tunnel to be dug there.

The plans for the tunnels were made. Now they had to make trap doors, so that the diggers could dig away in safety.

4 Hidden trapdoors

It was very important that the trap doors were perfect, or the Germans could find the start of the tunnels easily.

By 11 April Roger and Floody had chosen all the trap-door sites. 'Tom' was to start from a dark corner of the concrete floor by the chimney of hut 123. 'Dick' was to start from the wash-room of hut 122. 'Harry' was to start from under a stove in hut 104.

Minskewitz was the trapdoor expert. He was a short, wiry Polish officer in the RAF with a little grey beard which he was always tugging. He started work on 'Tom'.

The Germans had left some cement in the compound. Minskewitz used some to make a concrete slab, using a wooden mould. He reinforced the concrete with barbed-wire, and left some wire sticking out at the sides. He hid the slab under a mattress to dry.

Then he chipped a slab of concrete out of the floor of hut 123, where 'Tom' was to be. To make sure he wasn't caught, prisoners kept watch for ferrets outside the hut. These men on watch were called 'stooges'.

While they kept watch, Minskewitz chipped away like a surgeon at the concrete. When he had finished, his concrete slab fitted the hole perfectly. It could be pulled away by the wires on the edges of the slab.

Roger thought the trap door was perfect. He brought Massey, the senior officer with a bad leg, to look at it. Massey couldn't even see the lines where the slab fitted into the hole.

Then Minskewitz got to work on 'Dick', in hut 122. This trap door was one of the must cunning ever made in a prison camp.

There was an iron grating in the middle of the wash-room in hut 122. Overflow water ran down through the grating into a concrete well about a metre deep. Min-skewitz took off the grating and mopped out all the water with old rags.

Then he chipped away at one of the concrete walls, so that the soft earth behind was bare. He made a new con-crete slab to fit where the broken wall had been, and sealed up the slab with soap and sand. Then he put back the grating, and poured down some water.

It was a brilliant piece of work. The ferrets would never guess that there was a tunnel being dug under the grating. Later, the diggers could go through the tunnel as far as they had dug, shut the trap-door behind them, and carry on digging. There would be no danger of being found, because the rest of the team in the hut could fill the hole with water and put the grating on top again.

Then Crump started 'Harry's trapdoor, in hut 104. The stove in this hut stood on a square of tiles. Crump pulled off the stove, and took up the tiles one by one. He cemented them into a wooden frame, made by one of Travis's carpenters. He used this as a trapdoor.

But underneath there was solid brick and concrete. Crump had to bang away at this to get to the earth below. It made a hell of a noise. If the Germans heard it – and they were bound to hear it – they would be over like a shot.

So six men sat outside the hut, making baking dishes out of tin and wood. They made a terrible din, and the Germans never heard Crump at all.

It was a great moment when Floody told Roger that all the trapdoors were finished. It had been a big risk making them. But in these early days of the camp, the ferrets weren't well organized. The risk had been worth it.

5 Secret signals

Only a few dozen people in the whole camp knew where the trapdoors were. Yet almost everyone was working in some way on 'X Organization'.

A couple of days after the prisoners had arrived in the compound, notices were pinned up in all the huts. They said, 'Will those wanting to join a cricket team please put their names here.' 'Little X' in each hut told the men, 'It's not really for cricket, old boy, it's for "X".'

Each 'Little X' talked to all the men who signed their names, to see what they could do for 'X'.

Anyone who could sew went to join the tailoring section, led by Tommy Guest. They would make uniforms. The artists went to Tim Walenn's 'forgery factory', to make maps and passes. The engineers and carpenters went to join Johnny Travis.

Anyone who could do anything was put on the job best suited to him. All the rest became stooges (the watchers) or 'penguins'. Penguins were going to get rid of the sand from the tunnels – and there was a lot of sand to get rid of!

The 'X Organization' divided the compound into two parts. 'D' was the danger zone, where the tunnels and factories were. 'S' was the safe zone, the east half of the camp, where the gate was.

As soon as a ferret walked into 'D' zone, he was followed. If he got within 50 metres of a tunnel or 'factory', all the men stopped work until he'd gone off again.

Down by the gate sat a prisoner called the 'Duty Pilot'. The Duty Pilot sat there with a friend. He watched every single person who came into the camp, and made a note of the time they came in and the time they went out. He sat there for hours without a break, and never left his post until the next man came to take over.

All over the camp, there were warning points, to relay his secret signals. Next to him, there was a little stove, a Red Cross box and a coal scuttle.

If he put the coal scuttle on top of the stove, it meant that there was no danger from any of the visitors. If he put the Red Cross box on top, it meant that ferrets had come in: Danger.

By the back of hut 110 a man sat on a stool, reading a book. He wasn't really reading at all. His eyes were fixed on that little stove. If he saw the Red Cross box on top, he got up at once and closed some shutters on the hut wall.

A man standing by hut 120 would then blow his nose. And George Harsh, looking out of the window in hut 123, where 'Tom' was being dug, would see the man blow his nose, and tell his team to stop work. The trapdoor would be on in seconds.

Every factory in the camp had its own stooges and its own code of signals like this. There were nearly 300 stooges, working in shifts. 'X Organization' needed them all.

20

6   Sand is 'destroyed'

Floody and his tunnel team began to work on sinking the shaft under 'Tom's' trapdoor. The shaft had to go straight down for ten metres. Then, when the tunnel was dug, it would be out of range of the sound-detectors under the wire.

Floody had dug only fifteen centimetres into the dirt under 'Tom's' trapdoor when he came to the yellow sand. The grey dirt on top was only a thin layer, all over the compound. Everywhere underneath was bright yellow sand.

If the ferrets saw sand anywhere they would know that a tunnel was being dug. And with three tunnels, there would be about 300 tonnes of the stuff to get rid of. Getting rid of it would be about as easy as hiding a haystack in a needle.

Glemnitz, one of the senior German officers running the camp, was the number one enemy. He was a good soldier, with a dry sense of humour. No one could ever bribe Glemnitz – he was much too good a soldier for that. And Glemnitz had once said, 'No one will ever dig a tunnel out of here, until they find a way of destroying sand.'

Fanshawe, who was in charge of getting rid of the sand, thought for a long time. Then he had an idea. He told Roger that everyone must dig gardens outside the huts. Then the sand would be turned up naturally. Some of the sand from the tunnels could be mixed in with the garden sand and grey dirt. That would make it look natural.

'We can spread the rest of the sand over the compound,' he said to Roger. 'Then we can cover it up with some of the grey dirt from the gardens.'

'How on earth are you going to spread out the sand without being seen?' asked Roger.

Fanshawe had thought of that. 'With trouser-bags,' he said. And out of his pockets he pulled a remarkable gadget. He had cut the trouser-legs off a pair of long woollen underpants, and each end of a piece of string was tied to the top of each leg.

'You loop the string round your neck,' Fanshawe said. 'The trouser-legs then hang down inside your proper trousers.' At the bottom of each trouser-leg he had stuck a pin, and from each pin a piece of string led up inside the trousers to the pockets.

'It's just an idea,' he said. 'You fill the trousers with sand at the trapdoor. Then you wander round the compound, and pull the string in your pockets. Out come the pins, and the sand flows out at the bottom. If you're not a complete idiot, the ferrets won't see a thing.'

For an ordinary chap like Fanshawe, the idea was quite brilliant.

'My God, we'll try it at once!' said Roger.

'I have,' said Fanshawe. 'It works.'

All the penguins, about 150 of them, made themselves trouser-bags with pins and string. The Red Cross often sent out parcels of clothes, and most of the clothes were long woollen underpants! They weren't the most beautiful things to look at, but they certainly came in useful now.

Minskewitz was in charge of the trapdoor on 'Tom'. He stood at the top and spread blankets on the floor, so that none of the sand would be left on the boards.

Down in the hole, Floody and Marshall scraped up the sand into metal jugs, and passed them up to Minskewitz. The penguins took it out in shifts, hidden in their trouser-bags, and walked out into the compound.

A chap called Jerry Sage, a lanky American, organized combat drill in the compound. He had about 40 men at a time, leaping about and flinging the penguins over their shoulders.

The sand dripped out of their trousers, and was mixed

into the compound dirt with dirt from the gardens. More sand was poured down the deep earth toilet pits.

It worked like a dream, and the Germans never guessed a thing.

7 Collapse

An Australian with curly hair, called Willy Williams, was in charge of supplies. He took bedposts off some of the bunks, and smuggled them over to hut 123, where 'Tom' was being started.

When the shaft was about one-and-a-half metres deep, Floody put a bedpost in each corner, and slid bedboards in behind, to make a solid wall. When this was all secure, with sand packed behind the boards, he dug another one-and-a-half metres.

Then he put another lot of posts and boards into place. He walled up the whole shaft like that. As they got deeper, he nailed a ladder in one corner.

When 'Tom' was about three metres deep, Floody went to start 'Dick's' shaft, with another team. Marshall took over 'Tom', with three or four diggers. Floody and Marshall were both tall men, and worked very well down the tunnels.

They dug fast, because the sand was crumbly. Clay soil would have been better, because it was safe and solid. Sand wasn't safe. It collapsed as soon as you winked at it, so it was very important that the shaft was solid.

Just before sand falls, it gives a faint crack, and there's about a second to get out of the way. No one ever spoke much when they were digging. They were too busy listening.

In a couple of weeks, 'Tom's' shaft was ten metres deep. A few days later, 'Dick' reached the same mark. Over in 'Harry', Crump was almost six metres deep.

Marshall and his team began to dig out workshops at the base of 'Tom's' shaft. They dug a little room less than two metres long, where a digger could store his kit. On another side, they dug a small room to store sand in, until the penguins could get rid of it.

On the third side, they made a room two metres long. This was for an air-pump. The fourth side was the west side, facing the wire. This was where the tunnel would start.

Crump stopped work on 'Harry' to help Floody dig the workshops at the base of 'Dick'. They were both down there one day, with Conk Canton, when they heard a crack from the shaft.

Canton looked up and saw a broken headboard sticking out of the wall, about eight metres up. Sand was pouring through the gap. As Canton put his arms across his eyes, there was a tearing sound above. The walls of the shaft had burst, and the sand crashed down, breaking and twisting the boards lining the shaft.

By a miracle, the ladder stayed in place. Canton went up like a rocket, with Crump and Floody right behind him. Canton and Crump shot out at the top, and turned to grab Floody. They were just in time. The sand was up to his waist, and he couldn't move.

They were just able to pull him free. When he had got the sand out of his eyes, Floody swore for five solid minutes. He had a wide vocabulary. So now 'Dick's' shaft was full of sand to just below the top.

Floody went to find Roger, and told him the news. Roger said one extremely rude word, and was calm again. He was like that – he would lose his temper over little things, but when something big went wrong he was very calm.

'How soon can you start digging it out?' he asked.

'Crump and Conk have already started,' said Floody.

Within four days, 'Dick's' shaft was dug and lined with boards and posts again. Floody and Crump left Johnny Bull to carry on, and went to dig out the workshops at the base of 'Harry'.

That day, there was a new arrival in the compound. This was Wing-Commander Harry Day, known as 'Wings Day'. He had been shot down five days after the war started, and had been in several camps since. In one, he had met Roger.

Wings Day was a tall, thin man, with a thin face and hooked nose. He had a wild streak in him, and he hated being a prisoner. He had made escape attempts before, and had tried to tunnel out of a camp at Schubin. He had been sent to Sagan as a punishment.

Nothing could have pleased Wings more. As he walked through the gate, with armed guards on either side, he looked more like a hungry and unfriendly hawk than ever, and asked the way to Roger's room.

It was a great meeting. Roger told him quickly what was going on. He didn't tell him that 'Harry' was being dug in hut 104, but he just said that Wings might like a room there. He took him across, and Wings walked in just as Floody and Crump were climbing out of the trapdoor.

'Oh, God!' said Wings. 'Not here!' And he dashed off to find a more peaceful room.

It wasn't that Wings didn't like tunnels any more, but when you live in a room with one, the tunnel is boss. There are always people coming in and out, or keeping watch. There is no privacy – you're a slave to an ugly great hole in the ground.

Crump went back down 'Harry' with Johnny Bull to finish off the workshops. He was down at the bottom that day, listening hard, remembering his narrow escape from 'Dick'.

Suddenly he heard that awful crack again. He and Johnny Bull shot out of the trapdoor like champagne corks, and the sand thundered down. When it had settled, they found all the workshops and half of the shaft full of sand

There was nothing for it – they started to dig it all out again.

8   Tools and air-pumps

The prisoners were unshaven, with their hair cut short, and they looked a scruffy lot. But Johnny Travis stuck out like a dandy. The Red Cross had sent him his uniform in a parcel, and he pressed the trousers every night under his mattress. He ironed his tunic with a tin of hot water. he polished his boots, wore a silk scarf, and somehow managed to shave every day.

He had an idea that if he went round looking smart, the ferrets would never search him. The idea seemed to work, because they never did. This was just as well, because he was stocking up the engineer's workshop with tools. He usually had his pockets stuffed full of pliers, chisels and hacksaw-blades.

A man from 'X' called Valenta bribed a couple of German guards to bring in some broken files and bits of metal. The engineers sat for hour after hour, filing away, making chisels, screwdrivers, wire-cutters and knives.

Some of the knives were so good that they looked like the real thing – Travis spent 90 hours filing one of them. Soon the men's fingers were cut to shreds, but then Tommy Guest's tailors made them some gloves.

Willy Williams got hold of more bedboards, and had men pulling nails and screws out of the hut walls. It was a wonder that some of those huts didn't fall down.

Every other day, a gang of about 30 ferrets went into a hut after morning roll-call. They chose a different hut each time, and searched it from top to bottom for about three hours. They left a real mess behind – and usually they left all the things they were trying to find.

In hut 110 'Little X' cut out the inside of books, and hid chisels and pliers inside. Luckily, the ferrets weren't too keen on reading.

The outer walls of the huts were double, with about ten centimetres in between. In the little room opposite Roger's, Digger McIntosh moved a wall out about 22 centimetres. It was such a neat job that the ferrets would never see there was anything wrong with it.

A lot of tools were hidden away in this gap, through a secret trapdoor in the wall. Digger did the same to other walls in the hut, so that Roger had a dozen hidey-holes to store tools. One was in his own room.

Johnny Travis was always short of a good hammer. Then, one day, a huge horse-drawn cart came into the compound, driven by an old peasant. He had come to pump out the earth toilets.

A stooge walked up to the cart while two others started a fight on the other side. While the old peasant was watching them, the stooge pulled out the great iron spike that held one of the wheels on to the cart. He walked away with it, and the fight stopped.

The peasant went on with the pumping, finished, got back on to the cart, and drove off. At the first corner, the wheel came off. The cart wobbled for a moment, then crashed on its side, and the filthy contents spilt all over the compound.

Travis watched, with the iron spike in one hand. With the other he held a handkerchief to his nice clean nose. 'This spike will make a damn good hammer,' he said. 'But I'm not quite sure it was worth it.'

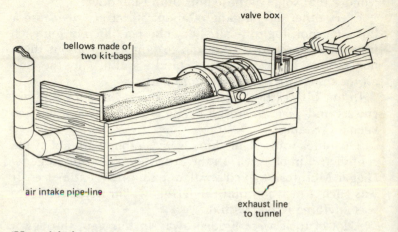

valve box

bellows made of
two kit-bags

air intake pipe-line

exhaust line
to tunnel

'Harry's' air-pump

There were now about 800 prisoners in the compound. But only a dozen knew everything that was going on – the rest only knew about the job each was working on. It was safer that way. 'Little X' in each hut told every new prisoner that, no matter what he saw going on in the compound, he was to take no notice.

'It's like this,' said Russell in hut 103 to a new prisoner. 'If you see me walking around with a tree sticking out of my arse, don't stare. I'll be doing it for a good cause.'

Even before all the tools were made, the men on the air-pumps started work. The bellows were made of kit-bags on wooden frames. The pipelines were made out of old powdered-milk tins. The tins fitted inside each other with the lids and bottoms taken off, and the joints were wrapped tightly with tarred paper. The men made metres and metres of pipelines.

The pipes ran from under the huts down to the pumps, which were by the spot where the tunnels started. Up in the shafts, an outlet pipe led off underground to the nearest chimney.

A pumper worked in half-hour shifts. He grabbed the handle of the pump, and pulled the kit-bags in and out, as if he was rowing. When the pumper pushed, air was pushed out of the outlet. When he pulled, air was pulled in through the inlet.

Now it was safe to shut the trapdoors as soon as the diggers went down the shaft. They could work for ages like this. Fresh, cool air was pumped into the bottom of the shaft, and stale air went up through the outlet pipe, and up into the chimney.

9 Keen Type

Roger had now been in different German prison-camps for about three years. One day, he was sitting on his window-sill, staring moodily across the hot compound. Valenta came in.

'There's a new ferret snooping about,' said Valenta.

'What's he doing?' asked Roger.

'He's under hut 122, with a torch,' said Valenta grimly.

'God!' said Roger. 'They're testing "Dick's" pump down there!'

'It's all right,' said Valenta. 'Everyone is stamping around their rooms. There'll be so much noise up there that the ferret won't hear a thing. But they're packing up just in case.'

Roger frowned. 'We'll have to be careful,' he said. 'This new ferret is a pretty keen type. He'd better go on the danger list. What's his name?'

'Don't know yet,' said Valenta.

'Well, we might as well call him Keen Type,' said Roger.

After evening roll-call the next day, the penguins got rid of most of the sand, but not quite all. Keen Type was in the compound again. He was a short man, with blond hair, a long sharp nose and a tight little mouth. He walked up and down and around the huts, darting in and out.

Suddenly, he walked straight into hut 123, where 'Tom' was. The man in charge of the trapdoor had about seven second's warning.

Keen Type just missed his promotion. He was just under a metre from the corner, where the trapdoor was being closed, when a door burst open. A body came flying through, followed by angry shouts from the next room, and crashed straight into Keen Type. They both fell to the floor, with Keen Type underneath.

It was the American George Harsh who had come flying through the door. He held his knee, his face twisted in pain, and tried to apologize. The ferret didn't speak English, and Harsh didn't speak German. Someone offered to translate, and a long three-way conversation went on.

Keen Type was too winded to show his anger, and at last, with an icy smile, he walked out of the hut. The man in charge of the trapdoor had had time to close it, cover it, and smoke a cigarette. 'Thanks, George,' he said. 'That was good timing.'

But George Harsh was swearing too much to listen. He really had hurt his knee.

10 Friendly ferrets

There was a prisoner who called himself Axel Zillessen. He'd chosen this name so that if he ever escaped he would travel as a Swede. In fact, he was a wool-buyer from Bradford, a tall young man with a hooked nose and a lot of charm.

Axel could speak German fluently, and he was such a nice chap that he could charm anyone. Valenta got him to make friends with Keen Type.

The next time Keen Type was walking across the compound, a stooge told Axel about it, and Axel walked out into the compound. He passed Keen Type a couple of times without speaking, and on the third time he said something about the weather. The same thing happened the next day. The third day, they spoke for about five minutes.

By the end of the week, Axel and Keen Type were walking up and down, chatting away for an hour. The next day, Axel took him to his room for the first time, and gave him a cup of coffee. The others in the room gave Keen Type a casual welcome. He sat among them with his hot coffee, a biscuit and a cigarette.

It was better than walking up and down the hot dusty compound, and Keen Type felt safe to grumble about the war to the British prisoners. He started coming in every day after that.

'What can we Germans do?' he said, after a week. He was sitting with his coffee and nibbling a piece of chocolate from a food parcel. 'Against Hitler and the Gestapo – nothing.'

'I'll tell you what you can do,' said Axel, sitting on the bunk beside him. 'You can accept that the Germans are going to lose the war and there's nothing you can do about it. When the war is over, we won't forget our friends. Start treating us as friends now.'

Next morning, Keen Type knocked at Axel's door, and put his head round the corner. 'Can I come in?' he said with a friendly grin.

He stayed for a couple of hours this time, and after that he came every day. Soon, he was quite friendly, and Roger took him off the danger list.

After that, Valenta got a German-speaking man to make friends with every ferret who came into the compound. The contact fed 'his' ferret with biscuits, coffee and cigarettes, and listened to all his grumbles.

'Why treat us as enemies?' asked the contacts. 'Soon you will want us as friends.'

Before long, the ferrets were giving away all sorts of useful information. Valenta put it all together with Roger. Soon, they knew all about the paths around the camp, the layout of Sagan town, the timetables of all the trains and the prices of all the train tickets.

They knew where the Swedish ships lay in Stettin and Danzig, what guards were around them, what guards covered the Swiss and the Danish borders, and a thousand other handy hints on how to get out of Hitler's Germany.

11 A network of supplies

One day, Axel said to Keen Type, 'Why do you make such a mess when you search the huts?'

'We have to,' said the ferret. 'We have to take everything apart, or we are in trouble with Glemnitz. Don't forget — you are our prisoners.'

'Don't forget you'll be *our* prisoners one day,' said Axel. He went on, 'It would be a great help if you told us when our rooms were going to be searched. Then we could have the place all tidy, and you wouldn't have to spend so much time going through all the mess.'

'You ask too much,' said Keen Type, shaking his head in fright.

But within a couple of weeks, Keen Type was telling Axel which huts were going to be searched in the next few days. After that, it was easy. Roger almost always got at least one day's warning of searches, and it was easy to smuggle stuff out of one hut and into the next on the list.

The contacts got a lot more than just information out of their ferrets. Soon, all sorts of supplies were coming into the prisoners' hands: pens, ink, paper, tools, German uniform badges, passes and money – all in exchange for cigarettes and chocolate. It was hard to get a German to take a bribe at first. But once he had done it, it was hard for him to refuse the next time.

Bit by bit the stuff came through all the contacts. They even got hold of radio parts, and made a radio. They hid it under hut 101. A couple of shorthand writers listened to the news everyday on the BBC and took it all down. Stooges kept watch at the doors as it was read in all the huts. The BBC has never had a better audience!

But it wasn't possible to bribe all the Germans. Glemnitz was much too good a soldier ever to take a bribe. His next-in-command, Griese, was known as 'Rubberneck', because of his long, thin neck. He was a real swine, with a dangerous temper. No one even thought of trying to bribe Rubberneck.

There were a lot of good Germans in the camp, though. They were just ordinary soldiers, with wives and families and homes.

The camp Kommandant was called Von Lindeiner. He was just over 60, and had been wounded seven times in the

First World War. He was a lean, good-looking man, his uniform always smart.

Even though there was a war on, he and Massey, the senior British officer, became fairly friendly. They respected each other. It was a strange set-up: politeness in the middle of a prison camp where every prisoner was in danger.

12   The underground railway

By the time the tunnels were about six metres long, Muller, Travis and McIntosh had the underground railways ready. Now the diggers could put the sand they had dug into wooden boxes on beech-wood trolleys.

These trolleys, with tyres made from old tins, were then pulled back along the tunnel on thin wooden rails, by a man at the bottom of the shaft. He pulled with a rope made of string. The boxes were unloaded, and sent back empty to the diggers.

Tunnelling now had a smooth routine. Each tunnel had a team of about twelve diggers, divided into shifts of four men each. After morning roll-call, each 'Little X' checked under his hut to make sure no ferrets were hiding there.

When everything was ready, a stooge went on guard, the trapdoor was opened, and down went the first shift of diggers. The trapdoor was shut again, and the diggers, dressed in dirty old underclothes, could work safely until just before afternoon roll-call.

It was hot, hard work. The diggers sniffed the fumes of the fat-lamps all day, and when they came up at night they did nothing but spit black. The air-pump did a lot to make

detachable air vent

lamp

air pipe-line buried below tunnel

trolley with sand-boxes

Diggers working at the tunnel face

this better, but it was still warm in the tunnel and the diggers were in a constant sweat.

Sometimes the ferrets walked near the trapdoors on top, and then the alarm tin in the shaft gave a soft rattle. The tin hung from one of the workshop roofs, and had a couple of stones in it. A string led from it up to the hut floor, and as soon as a ferret came near, someone pulled the string.

When they heard it rattle, everyone froze, so that the ferret would not hear anything. They lay there without moving until the tin rattled again as the ferret walked away.

At about 4.30, the diggers changed into their ordinary clothes, and tried to comb the sand out of their hair. When they got the all-clear signal from above, up they came, and the trapdoors were shut again. The diggers washed off any sand on the hut floors, and went on roll-call with everyone else.

After roll-call, each 'Little X' checked the hut again, and down went the next shift. The penguins came along and collected the sand in their trousers, and walked off across the compound. As soon as the last bag of sand was emptied, the underground men came up and the trapdoors were shut for the night.

When each tunnel was about ten metres long, Floody knew they would have to be careful with the wood which held up the top and sides. They were running out of wood. They began spacing the frames about 30 centimetres apart, and putting boards on top.

Every bed now had about three boards missing, and the mattresses sagged in the middle. The men got used to it in time.

With this new way of holding up the tunnel roofs, the falls of sand got much worse. There was hardly ever time to get clear: just the little cracking noise, and down it came, usually burying the digger from head to hips, and leaving a great hole above.

Over and over again this happened, putting out the

fat-lamps and filling the men's noses and throats with sand. And over and over again they had to dig their way out.

The worst thing was that the falls meant there was extra sand to get rid of. No matter how much they tried to pack it back into the hole, there was always extra sand for the penguins to carry away.

One of Travis's team made the lighting a bit better. He cut off bits of wire from inside the huts and fixed up a long cable from the shafts to the power lines in the huts. This meant there was electric light at night in the shaft and for the first few metres of the tunnels.

On a good day, when there weren't too many ferret alarms, or falls, each tunnel got about a metre-and-a-half further. By early June 'Tom' was eighteen metres long, and the other two were catching up.

13 Race against time

About 10 June, something like a hundred Russian prisoners were brought to the camp. German guards with tommy-guns stood by them as they started to chop the trees down outside the south fence. Then large convoys of trucks came and carted all the trunks away. In four days the edge of the wood was 45 metres further away. That meant another 45 metres to dig.

Massey went to see the Kommandant, Von Lindeiner, who told him that they were building a new compound.

'It is for the Americans,' he said. 'We are going to put them in a different compound.'

'Surely that isn't necessary,' said Massey. 'We speak the

same language. The Americans are our allies, and we get on very well.'

'I think,' said Von Lindeiner drily, 'that is why the new compound is being built.'

Massey sent for Roger and Wings Day and told them the news. 'There's nothing we can do about it,' he said. 'I think the new compound will be ready in about two months.' He looked at Roger. 'What are we going to do?' he asked.

'Well, sir,' said Roger, 'the obvious thing is to keep working on just one tunnel. 'Tom' is the longest. We'll go flat out on that. We can do it if we're lucky.'

That night, Minskewitz scraped out the soap that sealed the edges of 'Dick's' trapdoor, and put in cement. Crump put cement all round 'Harry's' trapdoor so that it was part of the floor again.

Roger and Floody picked the fifteen best diggers, and split them into three shifts to work on 'Tom'. In spite of bad falls of sand, by the end of the week 'Tom' was 30 metres long. Floody, Crump and Marshall built a half-way house. It was about three metres long, and about fifteen centimetres higher and wider than the main tunnel. They used longer boards to prop the walls up, and no rails were laid.

Two extra men could lie down in the half-way house, with just enough room to turn round. As the trolley came back from the face, one man lifted the sand-boxes off and passed them to his mate. The mate put them on a second trolley, and sent them back to the shaft.

Floody reckoned that the half-way house was just under the wire. Just over 25 metres further on was the edge of the wood. He and Roger agreed that about six metres inside the wood was a safe spot to break out of the tunnel.

'It's going to be very difficult to dig straight up for more than seven metres,' said Floody. 'But we'll have to do it somehow. It's too dangerous to slope upwards – one of the trolleys could slide down the slope and smash everything up.'

They were doing well, with no time to lose. They wanted to make sure that the Americans in the team who had worked so hard on the tunnels could have a chance of escaping before the new compound was ready for them.

14　The hunt

'Tom' had gone fifteen metres past the half-way house when one of the penguins slipped up. He was a bit careless, spilling the sand from his trousers on the outside of a ball-game crowd, instead of in among them.

It only needed a little slip. Glemnitz was prowling about, and saw the yellow sand before it was covered up. He didn't say anything at the time.

But the next morning, every ferret was in the compound, and they turned over all the gardens. In several of them they found more yellow sand than there should have been. Roger and Valenta watched them, and saw Glemnitz and Rubberneck walk out, grim and thoughtful.

Roger sent for the committee. 'Glemnitz knows there's a tunnel,' he said. 'Now there won't be any peace until he finds it. It's going to be a race, and we're on the dirty end of it. They'll search every hut, looking hard at all the concrete floors. There's nothing we can do about 'Tom's' trapdoor, except hope that they won't find it.'

For three days the ferrets searched hut after hut, but they found nothing. At the end of the third day Roger talked over the situation with Massey and Wings Day. They advised him to go ahead and start digging 'Tom' again – it was a risk, but a risk they had to take.

In the morning, Minskewitz carefully chipped away the cement round the trapdoor, and Floody took a shift down.

They dug three metres during the day, but the penguins had to be very careful now, and only got rid of three-quarters of the sand.

That evening, a chap called Birkland was walking round the compound. Suddenly, he saw a ferret hiding behind a pile of branches on the edge of the wood. He told Roger. They went with Clark and Harsh to have another look, and saw two more piles of branches. One of them was right on the spot where 'Harry' was supposed to come up out of the ground.

At two o'clock in the morning, Pieber went round every hut, waking all the prisoners, and doing a spot-check roll-call and search. Pieber made himself very unpopular, but he found nothing.

The next morning, Glemnitz found more fresh sand in the gardens by hut 119. He walked straight out of the compound, and by eleven o'clock a long column of a hundred armed troops marched in. They turned everyone out of huts 106, 107 and 123, and cut off that area of the compound with tommy-gunners.

Then the Kommandant drove in, with Broili, the Chief Security Officer. Also with them was an officer from the Criminal Police in Breslau.

A wagon drove up, and the soldiers unloaded picks and shovels. About 40 men started digging between hut 123 and the barbed-wire. They dug for most of the day, until they had a trench just over a metre.

Then they took thin steel rods about a metre and a half long and sank them through the trench, trying to find the top of a tunnel. They didn't have a hope! Once they hit something about a metre down, and got very excited. As they cleared away the sand, the Kommandant bent down over the trench to have a look. It was a rock. Floody, watching from a safe distance, almost died laughing.

Just before roll-call, the German soldiers gave it up. Trying not to look too silly, they filled in the trenches, and

40

left the camp. In the evening, Roger held another committee meeting.

'The heat is on,' he said. 'If they brought in a top man
from Breslau, they must be pretty sure we've got something
big on. From now on anything can happen.'

'Well, it's just a ruddy race, then,' someone said. 'We'll
have to cut a few corners.'

'We can't,' said Roger. 'It's too dangerous. If we cut
corners, they'll find something because we've been careless.
The main thing is that Glemnitz mustn't find any more
sand. How on earth are we going to get rid of it?'

And then Fanshawe rose to fame. 'Why not put it
down "Dick"?' he said.

It was so simple.

And that's what they did. In the evening of the next day,
the penguins carted all the sand into hut 122, and Crump
and two helpers dumped it at the far end of 'Dick'. They
took out the rails and frames as they came back, to use in
'Tom'.

In two days, the diggers in 'Tom' had dug six metres.
Glemnitz and the ferrets were still snooping about, but they
left hut 123 alone.

15 The fate of 'Tom'

Glemnitz found something else to keep himself busy. He got
in a team of men with axes and saws, and they started
chopping down all the pine-trees that had been left standing near the huts. They were all down in about three days,
and the compound looked naked without them.

This meant that any of the Germans watching could see
any movement at all around the huts. The stooges now had

to stay on watch inside whenever possible. And ferrets were still watching the compound from behind the piles of logs and branches in the woods.

'Tom' was going ahead very well, in spite of all this, and was making about two-and-a-half to three metres a day. Floody reckoned that in two days the tunnel would be under the edge of the wood. He and Roger were talking after roll-call one day about how to dig straight up into the woods, when Clark stuck his head through the window.

'Come and look at this,' he said, and took them over to the western fence by hut 123. More men with axes and saws were moving all along the edge of the wood.

In three days, the edge of the wood had moved back nearly 26 metres more.

The diggers and all the other members of 'X Organization' looked at the treeless ground in a fury. 'Tom' was just over 60 metres long. But now, it was still about 30 metres short of the woods. Pieber had told Valenta that they were building *another* compound.

And now there was more trouble as well. 'Dick' was full up with sand to the bottom of the shaft. Roger wanted to use the shaft for storing tools – where were they going to put all the new sand? It was too risky to put any more in the gardens, as the ferrets searched them every day now.

'I know!' said Roger. 'We'll put it in Red Cross boxes. Everyone keeps Red Cross boxes under their beds, for storing things, and the goons will never think of looking there.'

Floody agreed. They could put the boxes in huts 101 and 103, which had just been searched – that way they would be safe for at least a few days. Meanwhile, Floody gave up the idea of a second half-way house: there just wasn't time to build one. The straight digging of the tunnel went on as fast as possible, and they dug fifteen metres in five days.

Then Glemnitz searched hut 103 without warning, and a ferret found the boxes of sand. In half an hour, lorries were once again driving all over the compound, hoping to sink any tunnels. Glemnitz was told by one of the ferrets that two prisoners had been seen coming out of hut 123 with Red Cross boxes. Glemnitz searched the hut again, but gave up. After all, Red Cross boxes were a common sight.

But Roger knew that things were getting hot. He ordered Minskewitz to seal up 'Tom's' trapdoor that night. 'Tom' was now almost 80 metres long. There were still twelve metres to go to the edge of the woods, but the tunnel was already 42 metres outside the wire, and outside the light from the goon-boxes.

Roger and the 'X' committee thought it was probably safe to break out of the tunnel at that point, and crawl in the dark to the woods.

Then Roger had a new idea. He ordered all digging to stop for three days. 'I want to get Glemnitz thinking about something else,' he said. 'There's a faint chance we can make him think the whole thing is a hoax.'

He turned to an American, Jerry Sage. 'I want a gang of stooges,' he said, and he explained his idea.

Jerry rounded up 50 unwilling volunteers, and got them to hut 103. Then he gave each man a Red Cross box, and at short intervals he sent them in twos and threes across the compound to hut 119. Rubberneck soon noticed them and Glemnitz was soon in the compound, with guards and ferrets. With a stony face, he told them to search hut 119, and they spent four hours in there. All they found were empty boxes.

One of the contact men took Glemnitz aside that evening, and told him he was being fooled. He hinted that there was no tunnel at all, and that the whole Red Cross box effort was just to keep the Germans busy looking for something that wasn't there.

This partly fooled Glemnitz – but only partly. He ordered one last search of hut 123.

Floody, Roger and George Harsh stood and watched

from hut 122. They were grim-faced. The ferrets searched 123 for two hours, and the time went so slowly that it almost seemed to stop.

The whole camp was tense with waiting. Most people had an idea by now that something big was going on. Many months' work by many people, and many hopes, were hanging on 'Tom' breaking through.

And then, at about eleven o'clock, a ferret called Herman suddenly got his spike stuck in the concrete floor. He bent down to have a look. He could see the faint outline of the trapdoor, and he let out a wild shout of joy.

16   Discovery

Glemnitz was smiling with an ugly happiness. Even Rubberneck looked happy. They stood in the doorway of 123, waiting for Von Lindeiner and Broili. Behind them the trapdoor was still shut, because they didn't know how to open it, but they had scraped the edges clear and a ferret had gone off to get a sledge-hammer.

When Von Lindeiner came, they smashed the trapdoor in, and Rubberneck went down the shaft and looked up the tunnel. The only ferret who would go into the tunnel was a little grey-haired chap called Charlie Pfelz. It took him half-an hour to go right to the end, and crawl back.

Glemnitz stopped smiling when Charlie got back and told him how close the tunnel had been to the edge of the wood.

Roger was in a vile mood all day, but he snapped out of it in the evening. He, Wings Day and the committee held a three-hour meeting to plan the next move. It was a pretty miserable meeting.

Depression comes easily in prison camps. Some of the older prisoners had been working on tunnels for three or four years, and they were still stuck behind the wire, wondering if they would ever get out. It seemed hopeless.

The next afternoon, there was a mass meeting in the camp theatre. (The prisoners were allowed to put on plays here from time to time.)

'As most of you know,' said Roger, 'we started this plan with three different tunnels. We knew we might lose one or two, but we were sure we'd make it with at least one. We've still got two tunnels left. The Germans probably think "Tom" was the only one. We're going to lay off the other two for a bit, to make sure the Germans think this. Then we'll start again. I don't think they can stop us this time.'

After their first happiness, the ferrets didn't really know what to do about 'Tom'. In the end, Von Lindeiner rang the German Army engineers, and they sent along a tiny little man, with a happy but stupid face. He went down 'Tom' and laid explosives all the way along. It took him about two days.

Everyone got out of 123 and waited, while the little man pushed the exploder button. He wasn't a very good engineer. The charge roared out of the tunnel and up the shaft. A great mass of the roof of the hut flew into the air. The concrete floor blew to bits and the chimney tilted dangerously on one side.

The little man was sent away in disgrace, and workmen came in to repair 123. Even in death, 'Tom' had done his bit for the war effort.

Glemnitz made the mistake of talking too loudly in the compound to a ferret, and one of Valenta's team of German speakers overheard him. Glemnitz said he didn't think there would be any more trouble, because the prisoners must have used every scrap of wood to line the tunnel. If they ever tried to make another big one in the future,

Glemnitz would notice bedboards slowly disappearing.

Within an hour, Roger had sent Willy Williams round every single room, for the biggest ever collection of bedboards. In two days he had got nearly 2000, and stored them down 'Dick' and behind false walls.

A week later, the Americans were marched out to their new compound. They laid bets that they would break out of a tunnel before the British.

Glemnitz went with the Americans, and no one was sorry to see him go. But in fact it didn't help. Rubberneck took his place, and Rubberneck was just as clever and tougher as well. He was looking out for promotion, and he made sure the ferrets didn't get friendly with the prisoners any more.

Keen Type was told off for spending so much time in Alex Zillessen's hut, and after that it was hard to get any information out of him at all. Roger had wanted to open one of the tunnels up again after a few weeks, but now that the ferrets were so tough he decided to put it off. Meanwhile, all the other factories kept steadily on with their work.

17 The forgers

With a nice touch of humour, Tim Walenn had called his forgery factory 'Dean and Dawson' – the name of a British travel firm. It was impossible to get around Germany without having a fistful of permits and passes, and you couldn't get far without having them inspected by the cold eye of the police or the Gestapo.

Walenn had a very careful and precise nature, essential for a good forger. He had a smooth, calm face, and hid most of it behind an enormous moustache. Artists liked to work with him because he was always so polite.

His first efforts were faking gate passes and simple travel permits. A tame goon had got originals from the Kommandant's house, and Walenn hand-lettered copies with such care that they looked just like the originals.

In a room in the kitchen block, the factory grew, and more artists joined the team.

Bit by bit, Valenta's contact men got their tame goons to supply more and more originals, until Tim had quite a stock. He had a permit for being on German property, gate passes, permits to cross frontiers, about three different kinds of travel permit, and a French worker's identity card. All the papers were hidden behind a secret wall panel in hut 104.

It was quite easy to get identity cards from ordinary German soldiers and they even managed to steal an officer's card and copy it. But the trouble with these cards, and with a couple of other passes, was that they had photos of the owners on them. Tim told Roger that they must have photos of the British who were going to use the forged cards.

'We'll have to get a camera, that's all,' said Roger, and told Valenta. One of Valenta's contact men told the young soldier who had been supplying cards. The poor young chap almost fainted with fright on the spot. Valenta went back to Roger.

'We can't ask the poor little goon to smuggle in a camera,' he said. 'He'll be shot if he does.'

'Tell him,' said Roger, 'that he may be shot if he doesn't.'

The little goon brought in a tiny camera. Later he brought in some developing and printing materials. A chap called Chaz Hall set up a small studio in his room, and took photos of the prisoners who were going to use the cards. Tommy Guest made the German uniforms for them to wear while they had their photos taken.

Forging was a slow business. Tim threw out any forgery that wasn't quite perfect. One of the passes took a forger a whole month to make, working five hours a day. Altogether, Dean and Dawson made almost 400 documents. It was hard to believe it was possible.

The other factories were working hard too. Des Plunkett had a team of map-tracers all over the camp. Through the contacts, he collected all sorts of information about the countryside round the camp. He made maps showing the best escape-routes, down through Czechoslovakia to Switzerland and France, and through the Baltic to Sweden.

18 Clothes and compasses

Tommy Guest had his tailors working in different rooms all over the compound. Cloth was his main trouble. He took old uniforms to pieces and re-cut them to look like civilian clothes.

He got bits of cloth brought in from outside, and sometimes used the heavy linings of old coats. The only jackets and trousers given out in the compound came from the Red Cross. They were either old Polish uniforms, or the heavy serge uniforms of the ordinary airmen of the RAF.

Guest had a couple of people shaving off the nap of the serge with razor blades, to fine the cloth down. Then he dyed it – with beetroot juice, or a mixture of boot-polish and water, and once or twice in dyes made from the covers of books soaked in water.

He made a stock of paper patterns of different sizes, by cutting them out on sheets of German newspaper. If he didn't have the time or the cloth to make a suit himself, he would – if he was in a very good mood – lend the paper patterns. He usually did the cutting for the difficult suits himself.

There was one prisoner who wanted to escape on his own, and travel as a German railwayman. He asked Guest if he could have a porter's uniform. Guest measured him, and fitted a suit at one o'clock. By five o'clock the uniform was ready, complete with cap. The man would probably have got a long way with it, but the search-lights picked him up as he was trying to cut the wire.

Al Hake had his compass team in a room in hut 103. He made the compass cases out of broken gramophone records, heating the bits until they were soft and then pressing them in a mould.

Artists painted the points of the compass on little circles of paper which fitted neatly into the bottom of the cases. Then Hake sank a gramophone needle in the centre, and used this to hold the compass needle. The needle itself was made from a bit of sewing needle which he rubbed against a magnet. Valenta even got him some luminous paint for the needle, so the compasses could be used at night without the danger of lighting matches.

He got glass for the compass tops from bits of broken window, and cut it into circles under water, so that the glass wouldn't crack or chip. He made a little blow-lamp from a fat-lamp, and blew hot air through a little tin tube to melt the sides of the case. When it was soft, he pressed in the glass, and there it set, tight and waterproof.

He made one a day, and they were so beautifully done you would have thought they came from a shop. The best thing about them was the stamp on the bottom of the cases: when you turned one over, it read, 'Made in Stalag Luft III'!

As the maps, compasses, clothes and forged papers were turned out, Roger hid them behind false walls and down in 'Dick'. He realized that, although the Germans were very careful searching the huts, they never searched the huts of the outside toilets. So he hid a lot of the clothes up in the roof of one of them.

Von Lindeiner refused to allow any kind of communication with the Americans in their new compound. Massey put a semaphore signaller in an end room of hut 120, standing well back from the window, so that the goons in their boxes could not see him.

The Americans spotted the signaller in about two minutes, and put their own signaller in a window. They chatted away for half an hour every day. The British used to send over BBC news for a bit, but the Yanks didn't take long to get their own radio going.

The summer was a long one, and the weather stayed good for escaping. But Rubberneck kept the ferrets up to the mark, and the wood-choppers came back. They cleared the rest of the wood outside the west fence, and a new compound started to go up there. That ruled 'Dick' out for good, except as a workshop and store. Only 'Harry' was left now.

Roger kept 'Harry' sealed down. He didn't want to risk losing the last tunnel while Rubberneck was still so active. Autumn came suddenly, and Roger faced the fact that there was no chance of getting 'Harry' outside the wire safely before winter. Now they would have to wait until the spring.

'But don't think we're just going to sit back until then,' he told the men. 'We want "Harry" finished by the time the weather is right again.'

19 'Wire-happy'

With 'Harry' still sealed down, Roger organized 'wire-jobs'. Using cutters made by Johnny Travis, a prisoner would try to cut his way out of the wire, and escape on his own.

Anyone who wanted to try it applied to the committee. He had to convince Roger that he had a good travel plan, and had made up stories about himself that were good enough to pass police checks on trains and roads. The committee gave him a little money, passes, compass, maps, clothes if he needed them, and a pair of wire-cutters.

The man would wait for a stormy night or an air-raid, when the lights by the wires were turned off. Then he would crawl out of his hut, pray he wouldn't be seen by the guard with his Alsatian dog, and make for the boundary wire. There, he would try to cut his way out.

A couple of dozen people tried it before the winter, but there were too many guards and search-lights. One or two got clear, but only for a night or two. What usually happened on wire-jobs was that a man got clear of the huts, up to the wire – and back down to the guardroom with hands up and pistol in his back. Then he was put in the cooler.

Jacky Rae was a Spitfire pilot from New Zealand. He decided that wire-jobs failed because on dark nights there were always plenty of guards on watch by the wire nearest the huts. He thought there was a better chance if he got to the wire on the far side of the compound where roll-call took place. The guards would not expect anyone to go there at night.

This area was well lit by search-lights, but there was a slight dip in the ground. Rae and a Canadian called Probert got out of their hut one night and crawled on their bellies along the dip, with the search-lights flashing just above them. They were so careful that it took them seven hours to crawl 250 metres.

They finally got to the wire and began to cut it. They had about two strands of wire left when a guard saw them.

The Kommandant was so angry that he gave them a month each in the cooler. Probert hated being shut in, and couldn't stand it. He made a dash for the door one day, but a bullet got him in the shoulder before he made it. It was months before he got better and came back to the compound.

As the weather got colder, everyone had to face the fact that there was no point in trying to escape in winter. They would have to spend another year in prison camp.

Some prisoners had been behind the wire for three or four years by now, and the long wait was very bad for their nerves. The polite term for the way they acted was 'wire-happy'.

One man thought he was a General, and made everyone in his room call him 'sir'. The Germans took him away for treatment. Another man cut his wrists twice, but there is no privacy in a prison camp, and he was seen, and stopped from bleeding to death.

The Germans took him to the prison-camp hospital, but he got out of bed one night and climbed up on the roof. A guard spotted him, and shot him with a machine gun as he ran across the roof.

Another man was supposed to be taken away from the camp by train for treatment. On Sagan station, as the train came in, he pulled away from his guards. He jumped straight in front of the train. It had no time to stop.

Over in east compound, a man who could stand it no longer jumped over the warning wire and ran for the fence. He was tearing his hands to shreds on the barbed-wire when the machine guns put him out of his misery for ever.

By the middle of 1943 Germany was finding it hard to cope with the millions of prisoners and slave-workers now in the country. Himmler was trying to make Hitler give him full control of all prisoners-of-war. In October, the Chief of the High Command, called Kietel, gave out a new order. It said that from now on all prisoners travelling with guards must travel in chains.

About two months after the defeat of Italy, Von Lindeiner sent in some workmen who fixed up a loudspeaker in the compound. This was so that the prisoners could all have a dose of German radio.

The workmen were putting down hundreds of yards of wire. While they worked, they dumped a couple of reels of wire behind them. Roger got news of this while he was in the camp theatre. He sent Canton off with a gang of men to stage a fight, so that the workmen would watch them while the wire was being taken. They hid behind a hut, waiting for the right moment.

Just then the compound gate opened, and in walked a prisoner called Red Noble. He was just back from the cooler, and was carrying his blanket over his shoulder. As he walked up the path, he spotted the wire and a happy gleam came into his eyes. Without anyone seeing him, he picked up a reel of wire, put it under his blanket, and walked on.

A minute or two later, Canton and his men got going, and started a fight. The workmen stopped to watch. The fight didn't last long. Neither did the other reel of wire.

That night both reels were taken down 'Dick'. There were over 300 metres of wire – more than enough to put lights in 'Harry' when work started again.

The committee were really happy for the first time in a long while, but they were also worried.

'There will be a hell of a row', said Floody. 'Rubberneck will know exactly why we've taken it. Then the goons will start searching all over again, just when they're beginning to ease off.'

For once, Roger wanted to take a chance. As usual, he got his way, and all the wire stayed down 'Dick'. In fact, he was right to take that chance. The foolish workmen were too scared to report that they had lost the wire. They were to regret it bitterly one day.

Winter set in, bitterly cold. Roger wrote home, 'It can't last much longer. This is our last Christmas in prison camp.' But he could not have known how true this might be.

The compound dust was frozen hard under a foot of snow. Most of the men tried to keep warm by going to bed in the day-time. It was no time for escaping, and Rubber-neck knew it. The rest of the ferrets were very glad to go into the huts for a cup of tea or coffee, out of the cold.

20 Full-speed tunnelling

And that, thought Roger, made it just the right time to open up 'Harry' again. It was about 7 January when he called the committee together.

'The idea is a blitz campaign,' he said. 'If we can finish "Harry" in a couple of months while the goons aren't expecting it, we can seal it again and escape as soon as the weather is right.'

'But for God's sake,' said Floody, 'what about the sand? How on earth are we going to get rid of it with snow on the ground?'

'That's just what the goons will be thinking,' said Roger. 'That's why we've got to get going now. Anyone got any ideas?'

They talked about it for an hour, and got nowhere. In the end, they left to think about it, and broke up the meeting.

Crump and Fanshawe stood talking for a while outside hut 110. Suddenly Fanshawe said, 'What about the theatre? We could put the sand –'

'Under it!' said Crump. 'I was just thinking of that. We could put it under the floor – it slopes, so there's bound to be room. And the goons will never think of looking there.'

The next day, Travis fixed a seat in the audience so that it tipped back on its hinges. Under it, he cut a trapdoor in the floor. Fanshawe went down with a fat-lamp and found enough room to store all the sand from 'Harry' and more.

Straight after roll-call on 10 January, Floody, Crump and two others started to chip away the cement round 'Harry's' trapdoor. Crump had made such a good job of sealing it, that it took them about two hours. They lifted the stove off the top, pulled up the door easily, and went below, each carrying a fat-lamp.

Harry had been shut for about three months, and they were worried what state it would be in. But Crump had made a good job of that tunnel. The air was still fresh because he'd left the valve open on the pump. Only a little sand had leaked here and there, and four frames needed replacing.

Some of the pipeline tins had broken, though, and it was a long job to mend them so that air could be pumped easily. But on 14 January Floody was able to take the first full shift down for digging. He went up to the tunnel face in the trolley and felt the sand. It felt quite firm. He dug three metres that day, and back at the base of the shaft Crump stored all the sand in kit-bags.

After roll-call, the evening shift laid fresh rails along the three metres Floody had dug. And at about eight o'clock Langford opened the trap and got ready to pass up the sand.

It had never been so easy to get rid of the sand. As it was

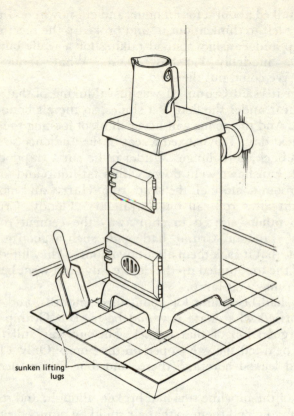

sunken lifting
lugs

Stove hiding 'Harry's' trapdoor

the off-season for escapes, Massey had got Von Lindeiner
to let the prisoners walk about between the huts until ten at
night. Hidden by darkness, there was no need to use the
trouser-bags.

As each penguin got to the trapdoor, Langford pulled up
a kit-bag full of sand on a sling-rope, and the penguin
swung it over his shoulder. George Harsh signalled the

all-clear from the passage, and the penguin nipped out, and went to the theatre.

A faint glow was coming out of the trapdoor there, where Fanshawe waited. Down below, a dozen dirty men in long underpants were crawling on their bellies by the light of a couple of fat-lamps. Each one took a bag in turn, crawled to the side of the floor and emptied it, packing it down hard. Then he passed the empty kit-bag back, and the penguin took it back with him, folded under his coat.

All the time this was going on, a team of stooges followed any German who came into the camp. George Harsh sat in his room with a list of exactly which German was where in the camp. If a ferret got anywhere near hut 104, where 'Harry' was, George went at once and told Langford. Langford could shut that trap and have the stove on top in about twenty seconds.

'Harry' was lit by electricity all down the tunnel at night. The stolen wire ran right up to the face, tacked to a corner of the roof. It made work much easier, though the day shifts still had to use fat lamps because the power wasn't on. Work was going fast.

21 'Sorry. Too late!'

'Harry' was almost sixty metres long when the full moon came. The sky stayed clear, and for a week the moonlight off the snow lit up the whole compound. Fanshawe told Roger it was too risky to take kit-bags of sand across the compound – it was like daylight.

Roger was impatient, but gave the pack-up order, and there was no tunnel work for a week. The moon faded, and digging started again. There were several bad falls of sand, but by 10 February, they had finished the second half-way house. It was nearly under the outer wire, and there were about forty metres to go until they reached the woods.

At the end of February, Himmler got even tougher with orders for treatment of prisoners. A new order was sent out: from now on, all escaping officer prisoners, except British and Americans, were to be sent at once to the Gestapo. American and British officers who were caught were to be kept in army or police prisons. The High Command would decide in each case if they should be sent to the Gestapo. If these officers were caught, it was to be kept a secret, and they were to be officially reported as 'Escaped and not caught'.

The men came off roll-call one morning and found tommy-gunners round hut 104, where 'Harry's' trapdoor was. Rubberneck and the ferrets were inside. Floody, Crump, Harsh and Roger walked round and round the compound, telling each other that Rubberneck didn't have a hope – and feeling sick with nerves.

Rubberneck came out three hours later, looking his usual gloomy self. He had found nothing.

Valenta had got friendly with Walter, the German librarian. He was a thin man with glasses, a rather gentle, harmless type. Walter told Valenta that Rubberneck thought there was a tunnel somewhere in the compound.

'What, in winter?' said Valenta, hoping to get more information. 'Where the hell does he think we can hide the sand?'

'I do not know,' said Walter with a shrug. 'It is nothing to do with me. But I think there will be more searches.'

'Where?' asked Valenta, and Walter nodded his head at hut 110. It was Roger's hut.

Roger took all the stuff from his secret wall panel that night. It was mostly lists of names. He hid most of them behind a panel in another hut – but, a bit carelessly, he carried the rest in his pockets. It wasn't like Roger to be careless, and he almost paid the price for it.

There was a search the next morning, but half-way through roll-call Rubberneck arrived with six guards. They split up and went up to different squads, one of them the squad from 110.

Roger could feel the lists in his pockets, and had a sudden idea of what was going to happen. His heart started to beat faster. He put his hands in his pockets and from out of the corner of his mouth he said to Conk, 'Stick around.'

Conk and two others moved up close to him, and as they did so, Rubberneck and Eichacher, an English-speaking German, got to the squad. Eichacher asked one of the men who their leader was, then called out: 'Squadron Leader Bushell, please. Come out and follow me.'

As he moved forward in the crowd, Roger passed the papers into the hands of those around him, and they passed them to others down the line. Rubberneck didn't notice a thing.

Roger joined a group of squadron leaders – Floody, George Harsh and Wings Day – and they were marched off to their huts. There, Rubberneck stripped them all naked, and searched them. He found nothing. Poker-faced, he let them go.

Walter had been right. Rubberneck searched 110 the next morning, and found a secret wall panel in one of the rooms. It was empty except for a little piece of paper with some writing on it. He passed it to Eichacher.

'What does it say?' he asked.

'It says,' Eichacher said nervously, '"Sorry. Too late!"'

22 Rubberneck on leave

Early in March, the chief of the Berlin Gestapo gave the 'Kugel Order'. 'Kugel' means bullet. The new order said that escaped officers who were caught, except British and American, were to be taken in chains to Mauthausen Concentration Camp. Mauthausen guards were told not to enter the names of these prisoners in the camp books, but to have them gassed or shot.

About that time, security police visited Sagan and talked with Von Lindeiner about how to stop escapes. They said that one way to stop them was to shoot any prisoners who tried to escape. Von Lindeiner later told one of his officers that if he was ordered to shoot prisoners he would kill himself.

Von Lindeiner sent for the senior British officers, doctors and chaplains in the camp and asked them to put a stop to all escape plans.

'It is not worth it, gentlemen,' he said, 'Anyone who escapes may suffer very hard punishment. The war may be over in a year or two . . . it is not worth taking unnecessary risks now.'

It was a pity he could not have said exactly what the punishments were. An officer in prison cannot give up the idea of escape just because the enemy asks him to.

Walter, the librarian, told Valenta that Rubberneck was going on two weeks' leave on 1 March. That was in three days' time. The committee could hardly believe their luck.

'We can finish before he's back,' said Floody. 'I'm damn sure we can, if we really get down to it. Then we can seal up the trapdoor and wait for good weather.'

He spoke too soon. Rubberneck struck the day before be went on leave. At morning roll-call, 30 extra guards marched up. Broili and Rubberneck were with them, and Broili went from squad to squad, calling out names.

Floody was one of them. So was George Harsh. Fanshawe was another. There were nineteen of them altogether, including a couple of the diggers.

Broili marched them down to hut 104, giving Floody, Harsh and Fanshawe some nasty moments, wondering if they had found out about 'Harry'. They hadn't, but the guards spent two hours searching the men. Then, without giving the men a chance to get their things, they marched them out of the gate. They were taken to a compound at Belaria, five miles away.

It was a stunning kick from Rubberneck. Three key men lost without warning, and at the critical moment! No one knew how the Germans had chosen these nineteen men. But Walter later told a contact that the ferrets had gone through the photos of all the prisoners, and picked out anyone they thought might be working on an escape.

Floody, Harsh and Fanshawe were really angry when they were taken away. They'd been working on that tunnel for almost a year; they would have been certain to escape, and now this – right on the point of success.

Later, they felt rather differently.

23 'Harry' is ready

Crump took over the next day as tunnel chief. With Rubberneck on leave the diggers dug like crazy. There were eight men down the tunnel on every shift now. There were two at the face; two in 'Leicester Square', the first half-way house; two in 'Piccadilly', the second; and the frame-cutter and pumper in the shaft.

The sharp-eared Shag Rees got a shock when there was a sudden rumble right overhead. He pulled back, expecting the whole roof to come crashing down. The rumble passed, and he realized it was a heavy cart above. They were underneath the road.

There were almost no falls of sand in the last stretch of digging. With Rubberneck away everything went smoothly, and there was still plenty of room under the theatre for sand.

In nine days they dug thirty metres. Rubberneck was due back in five days. On the tenth day Crump went backwards and forwards on the trolleys, checking the distance with a long piece of string. 'Harry' was almost 106 metres long from the shaft to the face.

There were 100 metres from hut 104 to the edge of the wood. Crump crawled out of the trap that night feeling that the whole thing was unreal. Almost a year ago they had planned for this moment – at last it was here.

'We've only got about six metres to go up' Crump told Roger that night. 'Unless anything dreadful happens, we should be finished by the time Rubberneck gets back.'

Digging a new shaft straight up was tricky and dangerous. The sand kept falling in heavy lumps, as Crump fitted the frames and bedboards along the sides. They fixed the ladder in sections as they went up, and stood on it to dig. It was back-breaking work.

Just before evening roll-call on 14 March, Crump hit pine-tree roots, and thought he had less than a metre to go. He came up for roll-call and told Johnny Bull, who was doing the evening shift, 'Test it to see how far you can go. I think you can put in a couple of frames and leave it at that.'

Bull went up the tunnel after roll-call. He was back in twenty minutes, shaking with excitement. 'My God, it's lucky I tested it first. I'd have broken right through.'

At a quarter to ten they were all crawling out of the trap, still with that feeling of unreality, unable to believe it was the last shift.

'Harry' was finished.

They brought up all the unused bedboards and pipeline tins, the kit-bags, the tools, even the sand-boxes off the trolleys. They burned them or hid them down 'Dick'.

Langford put the blankets he'd always used to deaden the sound under the trapdoor very carefully; he closed it, and sealed the edges with cement.

'Well, that's it, "Harry",' he said happily. 'Next time you open up you'll be useful.'

Crump went over to tell Roger it was all done. They both sat quietly for a few minutes, not talking much, but feeling very happy. Crump went to sleep that night still not quite able to believe it was true.

24 A moonless night

Rubberneck was back in the compound in the morning. He didn't waste much time. Just after lunch a squad of ferrets and guards ran in the gate and made quickly for hut 104.

Rubberneck walked down the corridor, opening doors quickly so he could see anything going on before there was a chance to cover up. He cleared everyone out, and the ferrets searched the hut for four hours.

It was the worst four hours the prisoners had ever known. Oh, the relief when Rubberneck walked out again, as solemn as ever!

'But we can't relax,' Roger said that night in the library-room. 'Rubberneck has got it into his head that something is going on in 104. We've got to move fast.'

'Well, we can't break out now,' said someone. 'Not in this snow.'

'We damn well can if we have to,' said Roger.

'It doesn't give the hard-arsers much chance,' said Marshall.

The 'hard-arsers' were those men who were going to escape on foot, instead of by train. It would be much tougher for them.

'They haven't got much chance anyway,' Roger said. 'You know as well as I do that most will be caught. We can't lose "Harry" just because the weather is tough. This escape isn't just to get people back to England. It's also to muck the goons about, and get them to take troops away from the front, to look for us.'

Roger had thought of just about everything. There were, he said, three things he wanted for the night of the escape. (1) No moon. (2) A wind to drown noise. (3) Reasonable weather.

The three darkest nights for the next five weeks were 23, 24 and 25 March. The 25th was no good because it was a Saturday, and that meant Sunday trains the next day – only a very few. They spent two hours talking, and didn't make any definite plan.

'We'll work towards the 23rd or 24th,' said Roger, 'and see how the weather turns out.'

He had worked it out that about 220 people, at the most, might be able to get out of the tunnel on the night of the escape. That ruled out most of the 'X' workers – there were about 600 altogether.

Roger and the committee picked 70 names from among those who had put in most work, and those German-speakers who had most chance of getting home. They put the rest of the names in a hat and drew out 130. Then they chose twenty more who had worked hard but who hadn't yet been picked. They were all to go in the order they were drawn out of the hat.

The lucky ones were told to get ready, and the committee picked marshalls to help them. Each marshall was given ten men, and it was his job to see they had everything they needed.

They began by making sure that each man had a fake name, and a fake story to tell if he was picked up. The marshalls gave them mock interrogations, firing questions about their home life, where they were going and why. They also found out what each man needed: passes, money, clothes, compasses, food and maps.

The whole organization was buzzing. They had several thousand German marks in the kitty by now, enough money for about 40 people to go by train. The rest of them would have to 'hard-arse' across country on foot. Most of them planned to make for Czechoslovakia – the border was only 100 kilometres south, though there were mountains in between.

Roger himself checked all the train travellers' stories, and gave them all the information he could on train routes and timetables. He gave lectures on German customs. Marshall and Crump told them how to get through the tunnel.

Travis's team made metal water-bottles. Plunkett got his duplicator going and made about 4000 maps. Al Hake had made about 250 compasses, and put them down 'Dick'.

Guest's tailors kept on working until the last day, and by that time they had almost 50 hand-sewn suits, really well made. These were mostly for the train travellers, who had to look the part. A lot of the hard-arsers were re-making old uniforms – it didn't matter so much if they looked a bit rough. Even if they'd set off looking really neat, a few days in the open would soon change that.

For some months 'X' had been collecting food from Red Cross parcels, and in a room in hut 112 half a dozen cooks were mixing 'fudge'. This was made from a mixture of sugar, cocoa, bran, condensed milk, raisins, oats, chocolate, marge and biscuits.

It looked like old glue, and it was taken over to the kitchen block and baked into flat bricks, then packed into flat cocoa tins. Each tin held enough calories to last a man two days, though it was hard to get past the ribs! The train travellers had four tins each, and the hard-arsers had six.

Stooges all over the camp were working overtime, and by the grace of God no slips were made that week. Rubberneck was still very much on guard, but almost all the huts had been cleared out, and the stuff was down 'Dick'.

Massey gave a last warning to those who were going down the tunnel. 'If you are caught, some of you may not be treated very well,' he said. 'I don't think the Germans would dare to shoot you, but please be careful not to take any unnecessary risks.'

In between lectures, Roger worked out how to get the 220 people into hut 104 on the night of the escape, without exciting the ferrets. It was two-and-a-half times the number the hut was supposed to hold, and they would all have to be hidden when the Germans came round to lock up. All those in 104 who were not going were given bunks in other huts for that night.

The forgers were working on papers morning and afternoon. They worked until their heads were splitting. Most of the men were going as foreign workers, coming from nearly every country in Europe. Tim Walenn was going as a Lithuanian.

'And what happens, please,' asked Marcinkus, who really *was* a Lithuanian, in the RAF, 'if the Gestapo get hold of you? How much Lithuanian do you know?'

'Not much,' said Tim, 'but then I don't think the Gestapo bloke would know any either.'

Dawn of the 24th was fair, and by roll-call the sun was well over the pine-trees, in a clear sky. The snow was shining and it was quite warm.

The committee met at 11.30 a.m. in Roger's room. It was one of the shortest meetings on record; certainly the most tense. There were only a few words spoken. People were looking up at the ceiling or sitting with their arms folded on the bunk, staring at the floor. Roger looked at Crump. 'How do you feel about it?' he asked.

'I think I can speak for all the tunnel men,' said Crump. 'I don't think we could stand it if we lost everything now.'

'Right. Tonight's the night.' Roger jumped to his feet. 'Get cracking!'

25 Ready to go

The whole camp must have known about it in five minutes. The tension was electric.

Langford and Crump made a beeline for 'Harry'. Langford chipped the cement away round the trapdoor, and Crump and another digger went below. They trollied up to the end with a load of blankets. Crump nailed one blanket as a curtain at the bottom of the exit shaft, and another about a metre back in the half-way house. They were to hide the light and any sounds when the shaft was broken through.

Then they nailed blankets to the floors of the half-way houses, so that people could crawl over them without getting their escape clothes dirty. Crump tore up more blankets into strips, and nailed them on the railway lines for the first and last sixteen metres of the tunnel, to deaden the sound of the trolleys. Travis came down and nailed boards on to the trolleys so that people could lie on them comfortably with all their kit.

Up in the compound there was a sort of organized muddle, as the 220 men got ready. So many things had to wait until the last day in case the ferrets found them. 'Little X' in each hut got his men together and gave them their water-bottles, fudge, compasses, maps and money.

He told each one the exact minute he was to leave his room, and where he was to report to the controller. They went back to their own rooms and started to sew all their kit into extra pockets inside their clothes. A lot of them had made little fat-lamp stoves, for making cocoa on the long walk across the snow.

They kept inside their huts as much as they could, so the Germans wouldn't notice too much rushing about. There were stooges everywhere. Tommy Guest gave out his secret store of suits to the lucky men who were going to escape.

The forgers, as usual, had the most hectic time. Al Hake had cut out a date stamp from a rubber boot-heel the night before, and now it was ready. Tim Walenn and his men went to work, stamping all the papers with the date: 24 March 1944. Then they sorted them and gave them out.

Crump came up the shaft for afternoon roll-call.

'Still got a hell of a lot to do,' he told Roger.

'Can you make it by 8.30?' asked Roger.

'I think we might just do it,' said Crump. 'We'll have a damn good try, anyway.'

After roll-call Crump and Langford went straight back to 104. The stooges searched the hut, in case any ferrets had hidden there. Then they gave the all-clear, and Langford pulled the trap door up.

'The last all-clear,' said Crump, and went below. He seemed almost sad about it. Crump and Canton were not allowed to escape this time. Massey wanted the expert tunnellers to stay in camp for the next time.

Crump carried a little box of light bulbs. He went all the way down the tunnel, and fixed up extra lights. He trollied back to the bottom of the shaft, prayed that they would all work, and switched on. The tunnel lit up like the Blackpool lights.

Darkness had fallen over the camp. People were sitting in their rooms, trying to talk about other things, feeling restless, and thinking only of the tunnel.

At six o'clock there was an early dinner party in Travis's room. No one talked much. Roger ate slowly, trying to relax. Someone broke the silence and asked him how he felt.

'All right,' he said. 'They won't get me this time.'

26 Moving off

At five to seven, a man in a rough black suit got up from his bunk in hut 107, and pulled on a coat that seemed to bulge in a few places. This man was called Richards, one of the hard-arsers. With a grin that was a bit too tight, he shook hands with everyone.

'Good-bye, you lot,' he said. 'Sorry I can't stay. See you in London after the war.'

'See you looking out of the cooler window in a couple of days, you mean!' said his 'Little X'. 'Good luck, old boy. Don't get your feet wet.'

Richards picked up a blanket, folded and tied, and at seven o'clock sharp he walked out of the hut, and down to hut 109. He went into room 17. A stooge was standing at the window, and a chap called Norman was sitting at a table. He had a list in front of him.

'On time,' said Norman. 'You're first. You can go right away.'

Richards went out of the hut, across the path, and into 104. Another man, called Torrens, was standing in the doorway of the hut kitchen, with a list in his hand. He checked off Richards's name, and pointed to a door.

'Room 6,' he said. 'Get into a bunk and stay there.'

Richards went in and lay down. He tried to relax, but he couldn't. He was wide awake, and on edge.

Every 30 seconds, all over the compound, people were saying good-bye, walking out in heavy coats into the dark, and going by different routes to hut 109 and then 104. Stooges were bringing Norman reports every minute on the position of every German in the camp.

So far, it was going like clockwork. Hut 104 was filling up fast. Then, at about quarter to eight, Torrens had a bad

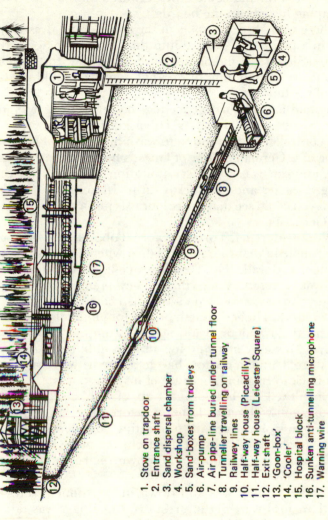

1. Stove on trapdoor
2. Entrance shaft
3. Sand dispersal chamber
4. Workshop
5. Sand-boxes from trolleys
6. Air-pump
7. Air pipe-line buried under tunnel floor
8. Tunneller travelling on railway
9. Railway lines
10. Half-way house (Piccadilly)
11. Half-way house (Leicester Square)
12. Exit shaft
13. 'Goon-box'
14. 'Cooler'
15. Hospital block
16. Sunken anti-tunnelling microphone
17. Warning wire

Escape tunnel

moment. The door of the hut opened, and he saw a German officer walk in, and come down towards him, his jackboots clumping heavily on the boards.

There were three escapers in the corridor, all dressed up, and in a panic they dashed into the nearest room. Torrens was terrified for a moment, then walked towards the German to try to stop him, or do anything that would get him out of the hut.

He had a sick, horrible feeling that everything was lost. And then he saw that it was Tobolski, the Pole.

A controller had forgotten to warn him that Tobolski was going as a German, in one of Guest's home-made uniforms. The uniform was a perfect imitation, with all the right badges, eagles and swastickas on it. If you saw it by daylight, you could see that the colour was just a little bluer than the German grey.

Weak with relief, Torrens waved Tobolski into his room. The people in that room nearly died when Tobolski opened the door and walked in. He was travelling with Wings Day, who was dressed as a civilian. They planned to make for Stetting and stow away on a Swedish ship.

In room 23, Roger, Marshall and Johnny Bull were standing by the trapdoor, waiting for Crump to finish down below. Massey came limping in. He didn't say much. A week ago, German doctors had told him he was going to be sent back to England, because of his bad foot.

'I can't tell you how proud I am of you,' he said quietly. 'I hope you will get to London before me. You know how much I'm looking forward to meeting you there.'

He shook hands. 'Now I'll get out of your way and give you a clear run.' He limped off down the corridor and out into the snow.

At 8.30, Crump was still down in the tunnel. Marshall and Langford were getting restless, but Roger was talking away quite gaily. A bit too gaily. He was going to travel as a French businessman, and in a grey suit and felt hat he really looked the part. He was travelling with a Frenchman: they planned to link up with an escape chain in France.

Up by the trapdoor, the minutes dragged like hours, and even Roger at last began to get restless. They were running late already. Langford went down the shaft and met Crump as he trollied back down the tunnel.

'For heaven's sake, how much longer?' asked Langford.

'All OK except the new rope on the end trolleys,' said Crump. 'Bull and Marshall can fix them on when they get to the end. Save time.'

Langford went back up and told them this at the top. And at a quarter to nine Bull and Marshall climbed down the ladder. Crump gave Bull the new trolley ropes and quietly shook his hand.

'Good luck,' he said. 'I wish to God I was going with you.'

Then the men at the top went one-by-one down the shaft, and one-by-one trollied up to Piccadilly, the first half-way house, and sent the trolley back for the next man.

At last seventeen men were in position, packed closely together. In the end half-way house lay Johnny Bull and Marshall, side-by-side.

Just behind, touching their feet, lay Roger and Scheidhauer, his French travelling companion. Then came Valenta and Stevens, then Dowse, who was to haul the next lot along the tunnel. In the tiny space they were packed like sardines, all waiting to go. Crump was there too, in charge.

It was about 9.30 when Roger spoke, quietly, as if they were doing an everyday job. 'I think you can get going now, Johnny. Dig up to the top. Everyone is in position.'

Johnny Bull grunted, and crawled carefully through the blankets. Seconds later they heard him climbing up the shaft in the dark. The idea was that he would open up, and then lie outside the hole in the trees.

The people following him were to climb up the ladder and stop, just below the top, so that he could feel their heads in the dark. When it was all clear, he would tap them on the head, and out they would go. Johnny was going to travel as a workman, so it wouldn't matter if he got his clothes dirty while he was opening up the top, lying out in the snow.

Down below, the men lay quietly. The air was thick and heavy, and they breathed slowly. They were running with sweat. They could hear Bull scraping at the roof boards with a wooden trowel.

He seemed to be scraping away up there for hours. Johnny Marshall crawled through the blankets, and called softly: 'How long?'

'I can't get the damn boards loose,' Bull said quietly. 'They're wet, and they've jammed.'

Time dragged by in the tunnel, and up in the hut everyone's nerves were on edge. People kept calling down from the trapdoor, asking what the hell was wrong. They should have opened up at nine o'clock: it was now ten.

After half an hour of this, Roger told Marshall to go up and see what was happening. Marshall went through the blankets and met Bull coming down the ladder. He was breathing heavily.

'You have a go,' he said to Marshall. 'I'm done in.'

Marshall took off his suit and climbed up in his long woollen underpants. He couldn't risk getting dirty and then travelling first-class. He tugged at the roofboards for ten minutes until at last one came loose. The rest followed quite easily.

He went down the ladder again and got dressed while Johnny Bull went up and gently scraped away the last few centimetres of earth on top. He suddenly felt the trowel push through the soil, and knew he was through. He scraped away a wider hole, and in a minute he could see the stars. It was a wonderful moment. He pulled himself up the last two rungs of the ladder and stuck his head up into the open.

He got the shock of his life. 'Harry' was too short! Instead of being inside the wood, he saw that he was out in the open, three metres short of the trees.

27 Outside the wire!

Bull looked back at the compound. The goon-box was only thirteen metres away. By the searchlight he could see the German guard's shoulders and his ugly square helmet, as he peered out into the compound, turning the light.

Bull felt naked out there. He climbed softly backwards down the ladder, crawled behind the blankets and broke the news. There was stunned silence.

It looked as if everything was a flop – 600 men working every day for a year, the escape-fever of those who had been behind the wire for five years. And now this. It didn't seem real.

Roger spoke first. 'Can you be seen from the goon-box?' he asked.

'I think so,' said Bull. 'It's dark, but a man lying out in the snow would show up plainly.'

They talked softly for a few minutes. No one wanted to put off the escape, when they were all ready to go. And in any case, Rubberneck would probably find 'Harry' if they put it off.

Then Roger thought of the vital point. 'All the papers are stamped with today's date,' he said. 'We've got to go tonight'.

He went on slowly, 'We've got to have a new way of getting people out without having Bull lie by the hole in the snow. Someone has somehow got to control it from the outside.'

And funnily enough it was the ferrets who gave the answer.

'Just a minute,' said Johnny Bull, with a sudden idea. 'You remember those piles of logs the ferrets put up in the edge of the wood, to spy on us from? There's one about three metres from the hole. Put the controller behind that.'

'That's pretty remote control,' said Roger.

'Tie a rope to the ladder!' said Bull. 'The controller holds the other end. When it's all clear, he gives two tugs and the bloke crawls out.'

It was the obvious answer, and Roger agreed on the spot.

He fumbled in his coat pockets and pulled out a pencil. Along the wall he wrote: 'Stop at the top of the ladder. Hold the rope tied to the top rung. When you get two tugs on the rope, crawl out. Follow the rope to the shelter.'

He spoke to Dowse. 'Warn everyone coming through about the new plan. Make sure they understand.' He looked at the others. 'Everything clear?' It was.

'Well, here we go,' said Bull. He crawled out through the blankets and climbed up the ladder, carrying a long bit of rope. He tied one end to the top rung and stuck his head carefully out of the hole. It seemed to be clear, and he crawled across the wet snow, trailing the rope, until he got safely behind the ferret-shelter.

The guard in the goon-box was still looking into the compound. He did not seem to worry about the woods behind – probably he never thought about looking there. His searchlight moved over the compound, up and down the fences, then joined with beams from other goon-boxes.

Bull heard a man coming along from the west, then saw him dimly. It was a German soldier, walking along the wire, carrying his rifle. He walked to the goon-box, stamped his feet and walked back. A few moments later another one came from the other direction, got to the goon-box and turned back. Neither looked at the woods or the compound. They just walked up and down, up and down in the bitter cold.

As soon as they were out of sight, Bull gave two sharp tugs on the rope. A moment later Marshall came out of the hole, keeping low, and crawled along the snow, touching the rope until he got to Bull. Marshall stayed with him for a few minutes, getting his eyes used to the dark. He put his lips close to Bull's ears, and said softly: 'Doesn't seem too bad.'

'No', said Bull. 'I think we might get away with it.'

The two wire-guards came into sight again. 'I have to wait until they've both gone before I can tug the rope,' said Bull. 'It's going to make it a bit slow.'

'Can't do anything else,' said Marshall. He waited until they had gone past. 'Well, see you in London,' he said. He felt for Bull's hand. 'Good luck, Johnny,' he said, and crawled off into the dark wood, trailing the rope behind him.

About 55 metres inside the trees Marshall came to the end of the rope and tied it to a tree trunk. He gave it a couple of tugs to let Bull know he was in position, and waited.

Back at the ferret-shelter, Bull tugged on the rope to the shaft, and Valenta came up, and joined him behind the logs. Bull told him that Marshall was in the woods, and Valenta crawled off, keeping the rope running loosely through one hand. If he felt a tug it would mean that the Germans were close, and he must freeze on his belly in the snow until the next all-clear signal.

He got to Marshall. A couple of minutes later Roger was there too. 'It doesn't look too bad,' Roger said softly. 'I think it will be all right. Off you go. See you back home. Good luck.'

Marshall and Valenta crawled for another 90 metres into the woods. Then they stood up and walked quickly away.

Marshall had his compass in his hand, and they followed the luminous needle, heading north. Less than 300 metres away was Sagan station. They were catching a train down to Czechoslovakia, where Valenta had friends.

Roger's French partner soon came out, and they waited behind two trees at the end of the rope until Stevens, the South African, got to them. Then they headed north, after Marshall and Valenta, while Stevens waited for his partner. So it went on.

28 Mass escape!

Back in hut 104 the tension had been almost unbearable. People kept calling down the shaft to Crump, asking what was wrong. Crump, worried stiff, and fearing the worst, called back: 'For God's sake, wait, will you? How the hell do I know what's happening?'

Just after ten o'clock, the lock-up guard went round the camp as usual, shutting and barring all the hut doors. He walked up to 104 and the stooges held their breath while he slammed the doors shut. Once he had gone everyone felt better.

Torrens set up a table outside the room with the trapdoor and settled there for the night. Now that the huts were locked the only person walking round the compound would be the guard with the fierce Alsatian dog. The extra men in the rooms now moved out into the corridor. Torrens told them to cover the floor with blankets, to muffle the sound of anyone moving about. Everyone took their boots off.

The corridor was an amazing sight: bodies lay all over the floor, and Tobolski, the Pole, in his German officer's uniform, stepped daintily in his socks over men in rough suits. Odd types in berets and cloth caps sat up by their blanket rolls and cardboard suitcases, smoking and trying to look natural. They looked, in fact, like refugees from the underworld.

At 10.15 Crump felt cold air on his cheek. Suddenly he felt better – the tunnel was open! He called softly up the shaft: 'They're through! Tell Torrens.'

It wasn't until 10.30 that the man on the trolley at the bottom of the shaft felt the rope tug as the hauler in Piccadilly gave the signal. He tugged back, and went rolling softly up to the half-way house over the rails, which Crump had covered with blankets.

Crump called up: 'Next please,' and a few seconds later a bulky shape came down the ladder. The trolley was back in a minute and another man lay on his belly on it and waited.

Slowly the movement got under way.

But it wasn't long before Crump knew that they were running even later. Roger had aimed to get a man out every three or four minutes, but in the first hour only six got out. The suitcases were the trouble.

The first 37 men were all going by train, and they almost all had suitcases. They found it difficult to hold the cases on the trolleys. Some dropped them, and some got the corners stuck against the frames of the tunnel. This was very dangerous, as it might pull out a frame and start a fall of sand.

Some tried to hold the cases out in front, lost their balance on the trolley, pulled the wheels off the rails and derailed the whole trolley. The derailing was the worst.

The tunnel was so narrow that the men on the trolleys couldn't get them back on the rails. They had to wait for the hauler to crawl down the tunnel, and lift themselves on to hands and toes while he fitted the wheels back on the rails. Then the hauler crawled back to his half-way house, and started hauling again. Over and over again the trolley would derail once more and the whole thing had to start again.

Crump turned round once to see who was next and saw not a man, not even a suitcase, but a trunk. Behind it a strange face was grinning: after a second or two Crump saw it was Tim Walenn, who had shaved off his great moustache for the occasion.

'Where the hell are you going with that trunk?' said Crump.

They argued for a couple of minutes – Crump knew it would never stay on the trolley with Tim, and in the end they sent it up on a trolley by itself and Tim followed.

A lot of the men had bad nerves by this time. Even some of the diggers who had been riding on trolleys for months found themselves getting stuck.

Just after midnight the men in the hut heard the sound of sirens, and they groaned. There had been no air-raid warnings for two weeks, but now, as the wail died away, they could hear bombs dropping on Berlin, 90 kilometres away. Almost at the same moment, all the lights went out.

Down in the tunnel it was terrifying blackness, and everything stopped at once. It was impossible to carry on. In the half-way houses the stuffiness, the fear of moving in case there was a fall, and the darkness, all became unbearable. Nerves were at snapping point again.

Wings Day, who was just about to set off for the Piccadilly point, stayed and helped Crump light the fat-lamps stored in the shaft. He took them up on the trolley with him. His nerves seemed as steady as rock.

He carried the lamps right through the tunnel, leaving one in each half-way house. But by the time the men were moving slowly through again, by the dim light of the fat-lamps, 35 minutes had been lost.

There was one good thing about the black-out. All the lights in the compound were off, and so were the searchlights. The guards by the wire were only watching the compound, looking for people trying wire-breaks in the darkness.

But delays had upset the plans of most of the escapers. Almost all of the train travellers had missed their trains. Some could catch later ones, but they wouldn't be as far away as they had hoped to be when the alarm was raised.

Up in the hut the whole floor was covered with bodies, huddled in blankets. Not many were sleeping: they were too much on edge. Almost all were hard-arsers and they knew they weren't going on any picnic. Walking across the snow would beat most of them, and there were bound to be a few Gestapo beatings.

By the windows the stooges saw the guard with his dog walk several times past the window of room 23. Everyone froze as he walked past, but the German never came near enough to look in.

29 Hold-ups

Crump had been praying for hours that there would be no falls of sand. At about 1.30 the luck gave out.

A big chap called Tom Kirby-Green was half-way between Piccadilly and Leicester Square when the back wheels got derailed. He tried to get off the trolley and his shoulders got caught on a broken frame and tore it out. The roof fell in and down came the sand, bringing another metre of roofing with it and more sand.

It was a bad fall. In two seconds Kirby-Green was buried from legs to shoulders and the tunnel was blocked. Wrapped in all his escape kit he couldn't move, but luckily his head was clear and he could breathe.

Up in Leicester Square, Birkland, who had been hauling him, felt the rope tighten and stop. He looked down the tunnel, saw nothing but darkness and knew what had happened.

He crawled down to the accident and slowly pulled Kirby-Green clear and sent him crawling up to Leicester Square. Then he started to patch up the tunnel, working like a sweating madman in almost total darkness.

It was a dangerous job, feeling his way as he tried to pack the sand back into the roof and put the boards back. It was an hour before he had finished, soaked in sweat and sand, and breathing heavily.

Just as he was finishing the sirens wailed again, sounding the all-clear. The tunnel was lit up again. Luckily, the electric cable had not been damaged by the fall of sand. Birkland spread out the rest of the sand between the rails for a couple of metres and crawled backwards to Leicester Square. The trolleys got moving again.

At about 2.45 the last of the men with suitcases went down. The rate speeded up a bit as the hard-arsers started coming through. They all carried a blanket rolled and tied on a string round their necks. It left their hands free so that they would be steadier on the trolleys.

But there were still too many delays. Some of the men hadn't tied their blankets as they'd been shown. They'd made the bundles too long, and the ends got stuck on the walls of the tunnel. Others had the string too loose, so that the blankets hung too far down and got caught under the wheels. This meant the trolleys got derailed again.

Crump climbed up the shaft into the hut and saw Torrens. 'We've only got about two hours now before dawn,' he said. 'At this rate, not even a hundred will get out. It's the blankets which are holding things up, so from now on – no blankets. The hard-arsers will just have to take their coats.'

'It's a bit desperate,' said Torrens.

'It's got to be desperate,' said Crump.

The hard-arsers were pretty good about it. Crump told most of them to go to sleep and forget about escaping – there was no chance now of getting more than a hundred out.

Crump went back down the shaft, and now there were no blankets things got faster. Then there was another fall in the second section and Cookie Long, now hauling in Piccadilly, crawled up to it. It wasn't a bad one and, working in the usual mad sweat, he fixed it in about twenty minutes.

After that there were no more delays, and men began to go through quite fast. At about four o'clock, Roy Lang, number 60, went through and took over from the exit man behind the ferret-shelter. He had just signalled two men to come out when he saw guards walking along the road. They were only a few yards from the hole. Lang couldn't work out what they were doing until he realized they were changing guard.

That meant another hold-up. It took twenty minutes for the guards to change, and Lang only got two people out in that time. Then the last guard went past, and the exits from the hole got faster again.

At 4.30 Lang jerked up his head in fright as he heard the goon-box guard shouting. He was looking over the side of the goon-box. For an awful moment Lang thought he'd been seen.

Then he saw that the guard was calling one of the guards by the wire. The wire guard went up into the goon-box and the goon-box guard came down and walked straight across the road to the hole.

Lang was almost choking with fear. The German was coming straight towards him. He was about a metre from the hole. Then he turned away, pulled down his trousers and squatted in the snow! For five minutes he squatted there, and then he pulled up his trousers and walked back to the goon-box and up the steps.

Lang breathed again for the first time in five minutes.

What had happened, of course, was that the guard had been looking through a search-light beam for hours. He was dazzled by it, and couldn't see a thing in the darkness.

Back up in hut 104, Torrens had ticked off number 83 down the shaft. Things were going quite smoothly now. Crump looked at his watch, and climbed up the shaft to check on the light outside. It was almost five o'clock, and it was getting lighter.

'Time to pack up,' he said. 'Get the next three down and that's the lot. If we can get them all out without being seen, the Germans won't know a thing until roll-call. That will give the boys an extra four hours before the hunt is on.'

Davison, standing by the trapdoor, hurried the next three down. The third and last man was just going up the tunnel on the trolley when a rifle shot cracked across the snow.

It came from outside the wire, by the tunnel.

30 The storm breaks

Just before ten to five a big, burly air-gunner called Carter had climbed out of the hole. He crawled past Lang and followed the rope into the wood to the tree where it was tied. He was to lead ten men through the trees to the road running south from the camp. This was how all the hard-arsers had been leaving, in parties of ten with a leader who knew the way.

A couple of minutes later Ogilvy, a Canadian, joined them. Then came Mick Shand, a New Zealand Spitfire pilot. Len Trent, who was next, had just crawled clear of the hole.

Suddenly, the sentry who'd been walking along the east side of the wire came into sight again For some unknown reason, he was walking on the near side of the road, along the edge of the wood. No sentry had done that yet. If he kept on going, he must walk across the hole.

Lang could just see buttons and cross-belts on his coat, and he went cold. He tugged sharply twice on each rope. Shand, half-way to the tree behind him, and Trent, just outside the hole, froze where they lay.

The German kept steadily on. He was nine metres away, and Lang felt his eyes standing out on stalks. The German was six . . . five . . . four metres away – and still coming closer. Still he hadn't seen anything. He seemed to be looking dead ahead, and not at the ground at all.

He was walking steadily through the snow, left, right, left. And then he put a boot down within a foot of the hole *and still didn't see it*. His next foot missed treading on Trent by a couple of inches. *Still the guard didn't see him.* It was unbelievable.

He took another step forward – and then he woke up. He must have seen the slushy track in the snow where the men had been crawling. He muttered something, and pulled his rifle from his shoulder and into his hands. Then he must have seen Shand lying on the track.

He lifted his rifle and was about to fire when Carter, who could just see the drama from the tree, jumped into view waving his arms.

'Don't shoot!' Carter shouted in German. 'Don't shoot!'

He gave the German the shock of his life, and his rifle jerked up as he fired. The bullet went wild. So did everything else. Shand jumped up and dashed into the trees. Ogilvy jumped up from behind the tree and ran off, throwing away extra kit as he ran.

As they vanished among the dark trees, Carter came forward – there was nothing else he could do. Then, right beside the paralysed guard, and still unseen, Trent slowly got to his feet. The guard saw him, jumped about a foot in the air, and then stood rooted to the spot, staggered with shock. He was a simple peasant-type and quite speechless.

A second later, Lang also stood up behind the ferret-shelter about three metres away. When the guard saw him, he could only shake his head. And then he saw the hole in the ground at his feet, and his mouth opened and shut like a fish.

For about three seconds he stayed like this, and then he pulled himself together, pulled out a torch and shone it down the hole. There was Bob McBride, hanging on to the ladder. He was to have been the next man out, the eightieth.

The sentry pulled out his whistle and blew it hard, then pointed the rifle at McBride and beckoned him out. McBride crawled out, and the sentry covered the four of them with his rifle. He was trying to speak, but no one knew what he was saying and probably he didn't either.

Lang heard the guard up in the goon-box frantically phoning the German guard-room by the gate. Along the road from the guard-room, about 200 metres away, a crowd of German soldiers came running. The man in the goon-box shouted to them, and they spread out into the woods.

The sentry pushed his rifle at the four men, and nodded down the road. They turned, hands in the air, and walked slowly off.

Back in hut 104 a hush had followed the shot. Around the trapdoor the silence lasted about three seconds, as the men in the room stood frozen to the spot, looking at each other.

Then Crump quietly made the understatement of the year. 'That seems to be a shot.'

'Of course it was a shot,' someone else said sharply.

'God!' Crump was the first to move. 'Someone's got it.' He turned to the man beside him. 'Davison, get the blokes back from down the tunnel.'

As Davison went down the ladder, Crump spoke to Torrens. 'Get everyone to tear up all their papers and destroy all their kit.'

He dashed over to the window, but could see nothing. He went back to the trapdoor, knowing that most people in the tunnel wouldn't have heard the shot, and would be still going through. A stooge called out that a mob of Germans were running along the wire towards the hole.

In fact, the people in the end half-way house *had* heard the shot. Men were hurrying like moles back down the tunnel. They climbed back up the shaft into the hut, and when the last man got out Crump closed the trapdoor and put the heavy stove back on top of it. He and Davison picked up all the blankets and threw them on the bunks.

Crump went out into the corridor. For one awful moment he thought the hut was on fire. There were fires everywhere as people burned their papers and maps and the hut was full of smoke. They trod on some of the compasses, and tried to hide others, and their German money, in mattresses.

A few jumped out of the windows – strictly against orders – and made a dash for their huts across the compound. The goon-box guard sent a bullet after one of them and that soon put a stop to it.

Suddenly everyone was still, looking at the door of the hut. They heard the bar being taken off, and the door opened. In walked the guard with the Alsatian. The guard was a simple soul, and didn't really know what to do.

He told a few people to go to their rooms, and mostly they took no notice. He walked up and down the corridor, collecting the coats and piling them in a heap by the hut door. The Alsatian knew what to do. He lay on the coats and fell asleep.

The guard could think of nothing more. He sat down near the coats and looked at his toes.

Now the game was up the tension lessened. About 140

prisoners sat around laughing and letting off steam. They
knew they would soon be searched and sent to the cooler on
bread and water, so they started eating the escape fudge. It
was too heavy to eat all at once, and soon no one could
swallow another mouthful.

Then Crump heard a faint scratching noise from under
the trapdoor. The ferrets had arrived. As they had found
their own way there Crump decided to let them find their
own way out again.

31   The search

In the guard-room by the gate, Von Lindeiner was standing in front of the four men caught at the tunnel exit. He
was red-faced, and his voice was high and shaky.

'So, you do not want to stay in this camp,' he said. 'You
wish to be out so the Gestapo will get you. They will shoot
you; get rid of the lot of you.'

No prisoner thinks of a Kommandant as a good man, but
von Lindeiner probably was. He was at least as good as it
was possible to be in Hitler's Germany. It was not his fault
if he could not give the prisoners enough food, or if someone
went wire-happy and was shot. And he knew that the
tunnel would be his downfall, and his own arrest could not
be far off.

At about six o'clock the first column of German soldiers
came through the trees from the camp headquarters. There
were about 70 of them, and they carried machine guns as
well as tommy-guns.

They spread out through the compound, closing the
shutters on every window. Then they made a silent ring

round hut 104. Four squads put machine guns on tripods in front of the hut doors.

Von Lindeiner walked straight into the compound, moving fast, staring straight ahead, still red in the face. Broili, his Security Officer, was just behind him, very pale, and trying to keep up. And then came the Kommandant's second-in-command, Major Simoleit, who had a shape like a starving gorilla. Pieber was with them, looking as solemn as an owl.

As Von Lindeiner got to the hut all the guards stood to attention, saluted, and drew their revolvers. Several guards threw the doors open and went inside, shouting for the prisoners to come out.

One by one the prisoners came out, wondering if the guns would open fire on them. Snow was just starting to fall and about a dozen ferrets were waiting for them. As each man came out a ferret grabbed him and made him strip naked in the snow. They made a pile of all the escape kit and clothes.

Von Lindeiner had his pistol in his hand now, and so did the other officers, as well as the ferrets. Broili's hand was shaking, but Rubberneck looked very calm. He was in a shocking temper, though. He knew, like the Kommandant, that he was going to have to do a lot of explaining.

All the men were still standing out in the snow. They were kept there for another two hours, while a check was made against photos to see how many were missing. When Von Lindeiner found out that 76 men had escaped, he walked out of the compound. His face was stiff with fury.

The 140 men marched down to the gate and there they stopped. Pieber stayed with them, in charge. He looked sadly at them through his glasses.

'Ah, gentlemen, gentlemen!' he said. 'You should not do this thing. It makes only trouble. The Kommandant is very cross. I do not know yet what he will do with you.'

He shook his head and turned away.

The Kommandant didn't know what he was going to do with them either. They waited another half-hour in the snow, and then a runner came up and spoke to Pieber, who turned to the shivering men.

'You can dismiss,' he said, and they turned and ran off to their huts. The rest of the camp was waiting to hear all about what had happened.

32 Hue and cry

Shortly after six o'clock that morning the telephone from Sagan had got Max Wielen out of his bed in Breslau. Wielen was area chief of the Criminal Police, and as soon as he realized how big the escape was he ordered a mass search throughout Germany.

The news was on German radio, and thousands of troops turned out on the search. The Gestapo went through all the trains checking papers. They stopped cars on the roads, checked hotels and houses and farms. The warnings went out to all the SS, the Army and the Air Force near Sagan, and for miles around old men and boys came to watch over fields and lanes.

Far away, in ports like Stettin and Danzig, the Naval Police were on watch for stow-aways. On the Czech, Swiss, Danish and French borders, the border guards were alerted. For a hundred miles round Sagan itself the country was thick with searching Germans.

It turned into the greatest search in Germany up to that time in the war. That morning, Wielen ordered Criminal Commissar Dr Absalon to find out exactly what had happened, and to write a report.

After crawling out of the tunnel. Marshall and Valenta had walked through the woods for ten minutes until they came out of the trees. In front of them was a narrow road, and

Map of Sagan and escape routes

right opposite, across the railway line, they could see Sagan station.

They walked up and down, looking for the entrance to the subway. They had been told that it led under the tracks to the ticket office and platforms. But a shed had been built over the subway entrance as a shelter from the weather, and in the dark they couldn't find the subway.

For some time they looked for it, and two more escaped prisoners came up, then two more. Before long, there were a dozen men walking up and down looking for it. Getting desperate, Marshall and Valenta pushed open the shed door, to see what was there.

Two trains had come and gone already, and then they heard the air-raid sirens. They were just wondering what to do when a German came out and shone a torch on them.

'What are you doing here?' he asked in German. 'Don't you know that the siren has gone, and you must go to the air-raid shelter?'

Valenta mumbled something at him in German, and they went back on to the road again. There, they decided it was too risky to try to go by train now.

'We'll go on foot to Czechoslovakia,' said Valenta. 'I know the way and I can get help there quite easily.'

They set off. Well before dawn they came to the Breslau motorway, about twenty kilometres south of the camp. They crossed it and as dawn broke they hid in some woods. They stayed there shivering all day, too tense to sleep.

At dusk they set off again, and walked along a lane, and through a small village. At the other end of the village three men suddenly came out of the darkness and before they knew what was happening a shotgun was pointing at them.

They tried to bluff it out, pretending to be French workers, but Marshall's bad French let him down, and the game was up. The Germans marched them back to the village, and phoned for the police from the nearest large town. Marshall knew then that there was no hope, and trod his passes, maps and compass into the snow.

An hour later a police car drove up and took them off to a small gaol. They were pushed into a tiny cell, where they found three other men from Sagan. At least it was a bit warmer in the cell, and they all ate some of their fudge, talked a bit, and fell asleep.

At dawn the cell door swung open. Half a dozen tough-looking police called them all out, pushed them into a car, and drove them back to Sagan. But instead of going back to the camp they were taken to the Sagan Gaol. They were interrogated, and pushed into a large, cold cell, full of bunks.

It was surprising not to be taken back to the camp cooler, and they began to feel uneasy. The door opened again after a while, and in came Ogilvy, Chaz Hall and two other prisoners.

Three times more during the day the door opened and more prisoners were shoved in. It was the same story with all of them. The snow had been too bad for them to walk over fields: they had had to take to the roads, and been picked up by German patrols.

By dusk there were nineteen of them. The guards gave them each two slices of black bread for the day, but no blankets.

Wings Day and Tobolski made it to the ticket office on Sagan station, and found it was half full of escaped prisoners. A couple of hours earlier they had all been talking in hut 104. Now, they did not even look at each other.

Wings Day and Tobolski went by train to Berlin, sitting apart, and joined up again in the crowds in the Berlin streets. They had the address of a Danish man living in Berlin, and found his flat. Next morning, they didn't like the look of his German girl-friend, and left. They spent two days in a bombed-out cellar.

On the Monday they went to the station to get a train to

a port on the Baltic. On the platform a man slid up to Day, showed him a police pass, and asked for his identity card. Day gave it to him, sweating. The policeman gave it a quick look and gave it straight back.

They got to Stettin safely, and after a day made contact with some French slave-workers in a labour camp. The Frenchmen took them into their huts and promised to find some Swedish sailors who would help them stow away.

They were waiting there in the morning when four German police burst in. The leader said at once. 'Where are the Englishmen?'

Day and Tobolski tried to bluff for a while, but five minutes later they were being marched off with hands in the air and guns at their backs.

The escaping prisoners were caught on trains, on station platforms, in barns, in villages. Tim Walenn's passes were good enough for ordinary times, but in that extra big search you needed more than good passes.

One by one they were rounded up. Two weeks after the escape, out of the 76 who had got out, only three were still free. The Germans never did find them. Two were already in England; the third was on his way.

33   Hitler and the Gestapo

Hitler had the first full Gestapo report on the escape on the Sunday morning, 26 hours after the break. He was at Berchtesgaden, and with him were Himmler, Goering and Keitel. When he heard the news, Hitler flew into one of his rages; he was having more and more of them now.

'They are all to be shot when they are caught,' he said flatly.

Goering protested. To shoot them all, he said, would be murder. And German prisoners in Allied hands might suffer because of it.

'In that case,' Hitler said, 'more than half of them are to be shot.'

That night Himmler spoke to his second-in-command, Kaltenbrunner, in Berlin. The next morning Kaltenbrunner gave out an order. It has since been known as the 'Sagan Order'.

It said that all escaping prisoners from Sagan were to be taken to the Gestapo for interrogation. After interrogation, they were to be taken part of the way back to their camp, and shot on the way. The shootings were to be explained by saying that the prisoners had tried to get away, and been shot.

That night the Gestapo chief in Breslau was told to form an execution squad. He chose a man called Lux to head the squad, and he and Lux chose half a dozen men to help them.

On Goering's orders, Kommandant Von Lindeiner was arrested on the Sunday morning. He was told to stay in his room. That same morning, Von Lindeiner heard that some of the escaped prisoners were in Sagan Gaol. He rang Dr Absalon and asked for them to be sent back to the camp. Absalon rudely refused. He said he wouldn't take any orders from Von Lindeiner because he was no longer Kommandant. Pieber told the camp later in the day that the Kommandant had had a heart attack.

At about midnight on Monday, the nineteen men in the

bug-ridden bunks in the big cell in Sagan Gaol heard tramping feet outside. The door swung open and in walked a bunch of evil-looking men with tommy guns. They were not in German Army uniform, but they all looked alike, in heavy coats with belts, and black hats pulled down over their eyes. Marshall thought they looked like Hollywood gangsters.

The prisoners were taken outside the gaol at gunpoint, and driven away, under guard, in a big covered truck. Marshall thought they were being taken back to the camp, but the truck kept going. They were all very quiet, and not too happy.

It was almost 3.00 a.m. when someone said he could see houses. Soon he said they were on a cobbled road in a fairly large town. Later, they found it was called Görlitz, but at that point they had no idea where they were – or what was going to happen. The truck slowed, went under a stone arch and a few metres further on it stopped.

The guards piled out, and made a circle as the prisoners got out one-by-one. In the darkness they could just see they were in a cobbled courtyard. On all sides were high stone walls, with little windows and bars. They must be in a gaol. A bad sign.

The guards pushed them at gunpoint through a door, along gloomy stone corridors and up two staircases. At the top they were pushed, four at a time, into tiny cells, about two metres by three.

There was a wooden platform in the middle of each cell, about a foot high: this was meant to be their bed. Worn out and hungry, the four men in each cell crowded together to try to get warm, and fell asleep. They didn't sleep too well.

At dawn they were woken by banging doors, and guards came in with their breakfast: a thin slice of black bread each, and cold mint tea. No milk. No sugar.

Funnily enough, everyone was in fairly high spirits. They hadn't any idea what was going to happen, and for the moment they didn't let it bother them.

They looked at their new quarters. Not much to see. Four bare stone walls of dirty white, a concrete floor, a thick steel door, and a small window, high up and heavily barred. It wasn't too cold just then, and they spent the day talking about what had happened since they crawled out of the tunnel. They were all hungry, but their spirits were still good that day.

There was no room in the tiny cells for a bucket to use as a toilet, but if they banged long enough on the door a guard came and took them to a bucket down the corridor.

The corridor was like a submarine – narrow, dark and grey, with steel doors down the side. The only people they saw were warders carrying bunches of huge keys for the cells. None of them was friendly.

Supper that night was two slices of black bread and a bowl of watery soup. They felt just as hungry afterwards.

Valenta was getting worried, but trying not to show it. He had done intelligence work before he joined the RAF and knew the Nazis better than the others did.

34 Interrogation

In the morning, guards came into the cells several times, and took out one prisoner at a time. Each man was interrogated, through an interpreter. 'Where were you going?' 'What were your plans?' 'Where is your kit – compasses and maps?' 'What information were you supposed to collect on the way?'

As each man came back from his interrogation he was put in a different cell, where he found other prisoners whom he hadn't seen since the night of the break. It was clear that there were more prisoners from Sagan there than just the nineteen from Sagan Gaol.

The interrogations went on for four days. Marshall had a bad time. As soon as he was pushed into the interrogation room, a heavy German got up from a chair. He walked heavily across the room, stopped fifteen centimetres away, and stuck his face out until it was almost touching Marshall's. He said, 'You will never see your wife and children again.'

This was not a good start, but Marshall knew it was meant to frighten him. He decided to play dumb. The interrogator behind the desk was a brisk man who shot out his questions sharply. After asking where he had been going, and what his plans were, the interrogator asked, 'What did you do with your papers?'

'Papers?' said Marshall, playing dumb as hard as he could. 'You mean the daily papers?'

'No!' snapped the interrogator. 'Forged papers and identity cards. Don't be stupid. What did you do with them?'

'Good heavens!' said Marshall. 'Did the others have forged papers? I wish I'd had some. Where did they get them? How could they possibly have got hold of identity cards . . .' He went on and on, playing dumb like this with all the questions.

Then came the question about his clothes. He was wearing one of Tommy Guest's best suits, dyed dark grey.

'Of course you know,' said the interpreter, 'you can be shot as a spy for wearing civilian clothes around Germany.'

'Oh, this is just a uniform I changed about a bit', said Marshall. He began to feel uncomfortable. 'You see, I rescued it, put boot-polish on it, and changed the buttons.'

'That is a civilian suit,' said the interpreter.

'No it's not,' said Marshall. 'Bring in someone who knows about cloth. They'll tell you it isn't a proper suit.'

The interrogator pressed a button on his desk, and his secretary came in. The interrogator spoke to her in German, and she came up to Marshall and rubbed the cloth between bony fingers, looking at the seams inside. She was a thin, sad-faced woman of about 40.

Marshall's face was hidden from the interrogator by hers. He smiled into her eyes and, a bit surprised, she smiled back. Then she turned back to the man behind the desk, and told him Marshall was not wearing a civilian suit.

She left the room, and Marshall answered more questions. Soon he made the interrogator so annoyed that he banged his desk with his hand and called the guard in from outside. Marshall was taken back to his cell.

After four days, when everyone had been questioned, the prisoners were all depressed. They had no idea what was going to happen to them, and they were very hungry. There was nothing to do, nothing to say, and by the fourth day they just lay in the cells, thinking about food, and what might happen to them.

A guard caught one of them standing on someone's shoulders, looking out of the window. He pulled him roughly down and told them that the next man who did that would be shot.

On the fourth afternoon, after all the prisoners had been put in different cells, Marshall found himself in with Royle, Ogilvy and McDonald, a Scot with a patient, lined face.

In the morning, they heard tramping feet in the corridor, and harsh voices. Cell doors were opening all down the corridor, and they could hear prisoners being taken out. Ogilvy banged on the door until the guard came to take him down to the toilet bucket. On the way down he saw six of the prisoners being taken out by several guards with guns.

One of the prisoners was limping a bit behind the others. It was Al Hake, the compass-maker. He said softly to Ogilvy that his feet were frostbitten, and he thought they were going for another interrogation.

'My God, those guards are an ugly lot,' said Ogilvy, back

in his cell. 'They look like the same lot that brought us from Sagan Gaol: same coats and black hats. They must be Gestapo.'

One of the men in another cell risked a bullet by getting on another man's shoulders and looking out of the window. Down below in the courtyard he could see the six men climbing into a covered truck, followed by the guards. Then the truck drove off through the archway.

Next morning, the four in Marshall's cell heard more tramping feet and shouting in the corridor and more cell doors opening. Looking out of the window they saw ten more prisoners being pushed into a covered truck with guards.

They sat around all day, nerves on edge, waiting for their turn, but no one came for them. That evening, when the cell door opened, and a guard brought in their soup and bread, Marshall saw a big 'S' chalked on the door.

'Good show,' he said. '"S" for Sagan. That must mean we're going back to the camp.'

'Maybe it means "S" for shoot,' said one of the others. There was a slightly hollow laugh.

That evening three guards came to the gaol and slept in the room opposite them. They told the men they were taking them back to Sagan camp in the morning. And at about nine o'clock the next morning the cell door opened, and they were taken under guard back to Sagan. There, they were pushed in the cooler for three weeks. This time the cooler was so full that everyone had company in his cell.

After a couple of days they found out who else was in the cooler: Rees, Noble, Carter, Lang, Trent, among others.

But none of the sixteen they had seen taken away in trucks from the gaol was there.

35 The Gestapo at Sagan

It was strangely quiet in north compound for a week after the break. The prisoners woke up every morning waiting for punishment, but nothing happened. As the days went by, nothing seemed quite natural, and they wondered what would happen.

Then, on the seventh day, the Gestapo arrived. There were about six of them, hard-faced men who walked into the compound and looked coldly at the prisoners. They had come to search the camp.

The Gestapo hadn't met Air Force prisoners before, and had no idea what they were like. They were only used to dealing with other Germans and the nameless victims they held in the gaols – people too scared to do anything against them. But the RAF prisoners at Sagan were under the command of the German Air Force, headed by Goering, and Goering wanted it kept that way.

The Gestapo sharply told the ferrets that they didn't need any help while they searched the camp. They dumped their coats and hats in the doorways of the huts, and prowled round the rooms.

Every now and then they came out with some of the nails the prisoners had pulled out of the walls, or a lump of iron they didn't think the prisoners should have. They made a pile of things by their coats and went back into the rooms.

As fast as they left things, a prisoner would reach round the door hut and take anything the men wanted to keep. The Gestapo didn't seem to think any prisoner would dare to do that.

One man got a bit more daring, and took one of the Gestapo hats. Then someone fished about in a coat pocket and rushed up to Conk Canton, grinning all over his face.

He was holding a little automatic pistol.

'For God's sake!' said Canton. 'Put it back. You'll start them shooting.'

Nervously, the man put the pistol back, and luckily for him he wasn't spotted. The Gestapo went off at last, taking nothing the prisoners had wanted to keep.

But without knowing it they left behind in the secret 'X' cupboards, a hat, two scarves, some gloves, a torch and some Gestapo papers. When they found out they were probably too embarrassed to do anything about it. The ferrets would have died laughing.

They went to the other compounds then, both British and American. Still they found nothing important. The Gestapo didn't want to admit they had failed, so they decided to search the Germans in the camp headquarters.

And there they had success at last! They found secret supplies of food and wine, brought in by a German pilot, and hidden by Kommandant Von Lindeiner and Von Masse under the cook-house.

The Gestapo got three more victims. They couldn't work out where all the cable used to light 'Harry' had come from. They checked the records of the camp electricians, and found that 250 metres of cable had been lost.

It was too late now for those two electricians to say that the cable had been stolen while their backs were turned. The Gestapo took both of them, and their boss, and they shot all three.

A new Kommandant arrived. The prisoners heard that his name was Braune, but they didn't see him in north compound. The punishments they had been waiting for came a couple of days later. Braune shut down the camp theatre, ordered three roll-calls a day instead of two, and stopped all Red Cross parcels.

There seemed to be something wrong somewhere. These punishments were only pin-pricks. No one could understand why things weren't worse. In the end they decided it was because the new Kommandant hadn't been in charge at the time of the break: he had no personal feelings about it, and he himself would not be punished.

Rubberneck was still around – he had managed to talk himself out of trouble. One of the ferrets told a contact that Rubberneck had said the tunnel couldn't possibly have been dug in the winter: there was nowhere to hide the sand in the snow. He said that 'Harry' must have been dug at the same time as 'Tom', and then sealed up while the prisoners waited to make the break.

Dr Absalon was making his report, on orders from Max Wielen, area chief of the Criminal Police. How, he asked Rubberneck, had so many prisoners got to hut 104 on the night of the break without being seen?

Rubberneck said that they must have dug small tunnels from nearby huts leading into 104. To prove it, he put on several surprise searches of the nearby huts. He found nothing, of course, but it gave time for things to calm down, and he was saved.

Blowing up 'Tom' had been a disaster. The German's didn't know how to destroy 'Harry'. In the end they poured sewage down the shaft in 104, and sealed it with concrete. Then they blew up the other end.

Rubberneck began to patrol the compound again, with a nasty gleam in his eye, but no one took much notice of him, except the ferrets. They looked very alert when he walked past.

The prisoners heard that Marshall, Ogilvy, Royle and McDonald had been brought back and put in the cooler. They saw two others being put in there too. Then there was news of eight more, then one another.

That made fifteen out of the 76 who had got clear of the tunnel. It was puzzling. No one could really believe that only fifteen had been caught, as things had been so tough for the hard-arsers. The prisoners thought that perhaps some had been taken to another camp, possibly Colditz.

Two weeks after the break it seemed that things were more or less normal again. The thaw had come, and now it was spring the men expected a British or American invasion at any time. Invasion would mean the end of the war. Release from prison camp began to look less like a dream and more like reality.

36 Murder!

On a morning in early April, Pieber walked into the compound and went straight to Massey's room. Massey was still waiting to be sent back to England. Pieber saluted politely, and asked him to meet the new Kommandant at eleven o'clock, in the camp headquarters. He asked Massey to bring his official interpreter.

'What does the new Kommandant want?' asked Massey. 'Is he going to tell us about more punishments?'

Pieber's face was very grave as he answered. 'I cannot tell you, Group Captain Massey, but it is something very terrible.'

Just before 11.00, Massey was taken out of the gate with his personal interpreter, Squadron Leader Murray. In the camp headquarters they were shown into the Kommandant's office. There was a carpet on the floor, a leather chair and a large desk, and photos of Hitler and Goering on the wall.

Kommandant Braune was standing behind his desk. He was a fairly tall man of about 50, with a lined, rather sad face, and thin fair hair. He wore the Iron Cross on his uniform.

Usually, when the Kommandant and the Senior British

Officer met, they shook hands. This time, no handshake. Braune gave a small, stiff bow, and waved Massey and Murray to sit on two chairs by the desk. Pieber and another German were standing by the desk, looking at the carpet.

The Kommandant stood up very straight, and spoke in German. 'I have been told by my higher authority to read you this report . . .' He stopped, and Murray translated to Massey.

Braune went on: 'The Senior British Officer is to be told that 41 of the officers who escaped from Stalag Luft III, north compound, have been shot. They were shot while trying to resist arrest, or trying to escape again after arrest.'

Murray could not believe what he had heard. 'How many were shot?' he asked.

'Forty-one,' the Kommandant said again. Murray slowly translated the report to Massey.

Massey listened in silence. He made almost no sign that he had heard, but he stiffened in his chair and the lines of his face went tight. When Murray had finished, Massey asked: 'How many were shot?'

Murray answered 'Forty-one.' He felt his face go bright red. The scene in the room seemed unreal.

There was a long, heavy silence. It went on and on, and Massey just sat there, looking straight in front of him. Then, slowly, he looked up at Murray.

'Ask the Kommandant', he said, 'how many were wounded.'

Murray put the question to Braune. The German looked nervously at a paper on his desk, and then out of the window. He said slowly, 'I think no one was wounded.'

'No one wounded?' said Massey. His voice began to rise a little. 'Do you mean to tell me that 41 can be shot while resisting arrest, or trying to escape, and that all were killed, and no one was wounded?'

'I have been told to read you this report,' said the Kommandant, 'and that is all I can do.'

Pieber and the other man were still looking hard at the carpet.

Massey asked for the names of the dead.

'I have not got them,' the Kommandant said. 'I have only this report.'

'I want the names as soon as possible,' said Massey.

'Yes, you shall have them,' said Kommandant Braune. Then he added quickly, 'I must tell you again that I am acting under orders. I can only tell you what is told me by my higher authority.'

'What is this higher authority?' asked Massey.

The Kommandant looked hopeless. 'Just higher authority,' he said.

'I need to know what has happened to the bodies,' said Massey. 'I must arrange their burial, and do something with their belongings. And I demand that the British Government be told of this.'

The Kommandant said that this would be done. Then he stood up. 'I think that is all, gentlemen,' he said. The two British officers stiffly left the building. As they got out into the fresh air again Massey said to Murray, 'Don't tell anyone about this dreadful thing until I have broken the news in the compound.'

Murray still felt his face was bright red. Neither of them felt like speaking.

On the way back to the barbed-wire Pieber came up to them. He seemed nervous and upset, and he said in a low voice: 'Please do not think that the German Air Force had anything to do with this dreadful thing. We have nothing to do with it. It is terrible . . . terrible.'

Pieber may at times have been a humbug, but not this time. He was a shaken man.

106

37 Breaking the news

Half an hour later, back in the compound, Massey sent word asking every senior officer in every room to report to the camp theatre. With this order went a rumour that 'something dreadful' had happened.

The prisoners were a bit uneasy, but it *was* only another rumour. Perhaps Red Cross parcels were going to be stopped altogether. God knows that would be bad enough. Camp food only just kept them from starving.

About 300 officers crowded into the theatre. Massey walked on stage, waited for a few seconds for quiet, and then said: 'Gentlemen, I have just come from a meeting with the Kommandant. He gave me the unbelievable, the shocking news that 41 of the officers who escaped on 24 March have been shot.'

There was a stunned silence. A lot of people felt suddenly sick.

Massey briefly told them about the meeting. He would tell the men the names of the prisoners as soon as he knew them. Just now there was nothing more he could say. There would be a memorial service on Sunday.

Still in a stunned silence the officers came out of the theatre. Within two minutes the news had spread, and horror lay over the camp. Life in prison camp was bad, but mass murder was something unknown. A lot of the men wouldn't believe it.

But there was no getting away from the fact that it had been officially announced. There was a memorial service that Sunday, and every man in the compound sewed a black diamond of cloth on his sleeve.

The Kommandant was afraid that there would be a revolt in the compound. He ordered the guards to be extra alert, and more ruthless if they had to be.

If any prisoners were a bit slow in getting into their huts at lock-up time, a sentry in a goon-box sent a spray of bullets over their heads and a few more round their feet.

Then at dusk one day, a German pinned a piece of paper on a notice board. Someone passing glanced at it, and gave a shout: 'Here are the names!'

In seconds there was a crowd round the board. A man at the front called for silence, and read out the names. There were gasps and curses as people heard their friends' names.

Then someone said: 'That isn't 41! It's 47.'

A dozen people counted the names on the list. He was right – 47! It was a terrible list. Roger Bushell was on it. That wasn't very surprising. The ever-polite Tim Walenn was on it. So were Birkland, Al Hake, Chaz Hall, Tom Kirby-Green, Valenta. Denys Street was on it, too. He was the son of a top British civil servant. The Germans certainly hadn't cared whom they shot.

When they knew the names, the men got back that feeling of stunned horror. Some of them were only kids, a year or two out of school. Some still thought it must be a bluff. Germany had been the first country, in 1929, to sign the Geneva Convention. This says that escapes from prison camps are understandable, and are not to be badly punished.

Two days later, another list was put up. It had just three names on it: Tobolski, the Pole who had dressed up as a German officer, and two others. That made 50.

A few days later a group of prisoners who had been badly wounded when they were shot down were sent back to England. Massey was at last among them.

The rest were left to puzzle over how the 50 had been chosen. There seemed to be no reason. Al Hake, for instance, had badly frost-bitten feet. He had no chance of trying to escape again, yet he'd been shot.

Then the Germans brought back some of the kit of the 50 – photos, and things like that. Some were blood-stained.

Two weeks later no one thought any longer that the shootings were a bluff. The ashes of the 50 came back to the camp in urns. There was no need to ask why the bodies had been cremated. It had destroyed the evidence of how the men had died.

On each urn was written the name of the place where the man had died. Four were marked 'Danzig' – only four men had been heading there. Other place-names were marked, but still there was nothing that the 50 had had in common. Why had they been chosen?

The only clue was the round number of 50. It was pretty clear that the Germans had just taken 50 and shot them as an example. God knows, under Hitler something like that was quite possible.

There was only one bright spot in the whole affair. The prisoners put bits and pieces of information together. They worked out that no less than five million Germans had spent time looking for the escaped men. That meant that the escape had been a kind of success – but at what a cost. . . .

The Kommandant got some stone for the men, and let a working party go to a nearby graveyard to build a grave for the urns. There was already a row of graves there where other victims from the camp had been buried.

Fifty were dead. Fifteen had come back. What had happened to the other eleven?

38 Some got home

In June a letter came in the prisoners' mail, signed with two false names. These names had been arranged before the escape. Rocky Rockland and Jens Muller had made it back to England!

Travelling by train, they had got to a town near Frankfurt the morning after the break, and changed trains there. By the evening they were in Stettin, the port across the Baltic sea from Sweden. Everything went smoothly.

They met some Swedish sailors who hid them on board their ship. The Germans searched the ship just before it sailed, but did not find the two stow-aways. At dawn the next day they landed in Sweden, and a few days later the RAF flew them back to England. It was the perfect escape.

Weeks later, another letter arrived, signed with another false name. Bob Van Der Stok had made it, too.

Van Der Stok, number eighteen out of the tunnel, had travelled alone. He wore a dark-blue Australian Air Force coat, Dutch naval trousers and a beret. As he came out of the woods by the station he was stopped by a German.

'Don't you know there's an air-raid on?' said the German. 'You should be in the shelter.'

Van Der Stok said he was a Dutch worker and didn't know where the shelter was. The German kindly took him right on to the platform at the station and said good-bye with a friendly smile.

Van Der Stok bought his ticket to Breslau, and was glad the train was so full: there was no room for the security police to walk up and down checking papers. By 4.00 a.m. he was in Breslau, and bought a ticket all the way to Holland.

At the Dutch border the Gestapo looked very closely at

his papers, but they let him through. Thirty-six hours after climbing out of the tunnel he was in Utrecht, his home in Holland before the war.

He knew that his mother, his fiancée and at least one brother were still there, but he didn't dare go and visit them. He knew that once the news of the escape got out the Gestapo would be watching the house.

Instead, he found some old friends in the town, and they hid him in a house two streets away from his old home. He was there for six weeks while they arranged the rest of his journey with the Resistance.

A couple of times he walked past his old home, and once he thought he saw the girl he wanted to marry behind a curtain. He walked on. The Gestapo *were* watching the house. They searched it at about this time to see if he was hiding, and took his brother instead, and shot him.

After six weeks the Resistance took Van Der Stok to the south of Holland, and smuggled him into Belgium in a little boat. On the other side they gave him a bicycle and he went off to Brussels. There, he lived with a Dutch family for another six weeks.

The Resistance then put him on a train for Paris, and he travelled now as a worker for a big Belgian company. It was just before the invasion, and the train stopped on the way to Paris when the sirens sounded. It was just as well. The Americans were bombing the next station into the ground.

Van Der Stok had been told to make for Toulouse. At a station in Paris, where he bought his ticket, they told him he must get it stamped at a German control on the station.

He took it to the German, who said: 'You must have a special permit to go to Toulouse before I can stamp this.'

'I've *got* a permit,' Van Der Stok said. 'If I hadn't, how could I have got this ticket?'

'Oh,' said the German. 'Of course.' And he stamped it.

In Toulouse Van Der Stok found a group of guides who were taking refugees across the mountains to Spain – for a price. He sold his watch for 10,000 francs, gave them the money, and was taken to a farm high up in the mountains.

There were 27 men on this farm: two Dutchmen, two American pilots, two Canadians and 21 German Jews. That night Van Der Stok made contact with a group of French bandits on a nearby hill. They would guide them to the Spanish border.

The bandits did not trust the refugees, and they made them walk in single file, at gunpoint. After a while they stopped, and the bandits pointed to a dip in the mountains.

'Beyond that,' they said, 'is Spain. Good luck.' They left them.

A few days later Van Der Stok was in Madrid. The British Consul had him flown back to England. It was just four months since he had crawled out of the tunnel.

39   And the others?

So eight were still missing. It wasn't until after the war that the Sagan prisoners knew what had happened to them. Plunkett and two Czechs were in concentration camps in Czechoslovakia.

Wings Day and Tobolski, who had got as far as Stettin, had been taken to the police chief there. He was quite friendly. He told them that a young Frenchman in the labour camp where they'd been found had got 1000 marks for informing on them to the police.

'That's a dirty trick,' said Wings. 'I'd like to wring his neck.'

'Don't worry,' said the police chief. 'When we have no more use for him, we'll tip off his friends about him. They'll wring his neck for you.'

Day and Tobolski were taken by train to Berlin. There, on the station platform, Tobolski was taken away. Wings didn't see him again.

Wings was taken by car to a concentration camp, an hour's drive north of Berlin. This was Sachsenhausen concentration camp, and the wire all round it was electrified. There was a wall outside the wire, two metres high. There were no ferrets there. They had never been needed. No one had ever got out from Sachsenhausen, except in a coffin.

Wings was pushed into a small compound just inside the wall. There he found three friends from Sagan: Johnny Dodge (the 'Dodger'), Dowse and James. There was another British officer there, Colonel Jack Churchill.

Two weeks later, the five Britons started tunnelling. They cut a trapdoor under Dowse's bed and worked in the dark all the time. There were no fat-lamps here. The soil was firm, unlike the sand at Sagan, so they didn't have to line the tunnel with boards. It was just as well, because they didn't have any boards to line it with.

And as far as they knew there were no microphones under the wire, so the tunnel was quite shallow, less than two metres deep. That tunnel would have been found in a week in Sagan. Here, they kept at it for four months, and by August it was almost 30 metres long. They thought they must be outside the wire by now.

Then one day Wings was in the toilet and saw a sheet from a German newspaper there. It was weeks old. He felt his blood run cold as he read a story at the top of the page. It said that 50 escaped prisoners from Sagan had been shot while resisting arrest or trying to escape again.

The five held a meeting in Dowse's room. They voted to take a chance and carry on. The idea was to try to get news back to England of the thousands of prisoners in Sachsenhausen who would probably be shot. It was a brave vote.

They waited for the right time, and early in September

there was a moonless night, with a light rain. At about eleven o'clock they came up out of the tunnel outside the wire. They helped each other over the wall and went off into the darkness.

They were making for a town south of Berlin. An Irish prisoner had given them an address there.

Wings Day and Dowse travelled together. In the darkness, they asked a man the way to the nearest railway station. Only then did they see he was a policeman. They made a dash for it.

At dawn they found the station and got the first train to Berlin. They changed trains, and got to the town they were aiming for. They spent the night in the cellar of a bombed house.

Someone must have seen them going in. The house was soon surrounded by Germans with guns, and then the police arrived.

They spent a couple of nights in handcuffs in a Berlin Gestapo gaol, waiting for the firing squad. They were driven away from the gaol, all the time waiting to be taken out of the car and shot.

But in fact they were taken back to Sachsenhausen. There, each was locked in a tiny cell to spend five months alone, in chains. Churchill and James had also been caught, and were in cells near them.

The Dodger had an amazing time. He was travelling alone, and jumped on a goods train on the night of the break. At dawn the next day he was miles from Sachsenhausen, and he jumped off the train and spent the day sleeping among trees near a little stream.

All next day he walked north-west in pouring rain, and just outside a village he met two friendly French slave-workers. They hid him in a barn for a week and brought him food.

At the end of the week the Frenchmen moved him to another barn, because they said he had been seen by a Pole whom they didn't trust. They kept moving him – to a huge rabbit-hutch, and then to a hayloft.

The Dodger spent a week in that hayloft, listening to the pigs underneath. Once or twice he saw the German farmer walking by with his shotgun under his arm. The Frenchman brought him food every day, and the German must have seen them.

On the seventh morning the Dodger woke up to find the farmer pointing a gun at him. Soon after, the local policeman came up. When the farmer had gone, he told the Dodger that he was sorry he had to arrest him. If he didn't, he would be shot himself. He gave the Dodger hot oatcakes made by his wife. He showed him a copy of the German *Police Gazette*, and there inside was a photo of the Dodger, taken four years ago when he had been shot down.

The second-in-command at Sachsenhausen came by car with guards and handcuffs to take him back to the camp. They put him in a cell by himself near Day and the others.

The five months in those lonely cells were miserable. They heard nothing of the war except bits of information from the guards about how well the Germans were doing. The guards made it sound as if the war might go on for ever.

40 The go-between

On 3 February, they opened the Dodger's cell and led him outside. A young German officer helped him into a car, got in with him, and off they drove to Berlin. What happened next was like a dream.

The young officer took the Dodger into a shop and bought him a whole outfit of civilian clothes: a suit, shirts, socks, shoes, a hat – the lot.

Then he took him to a flat, and introduced him to the family who lived there: an SS major, his wife and child. He showed him into a very pretty bedroom.

'This will be your room,' said the young officer. To the Dodger, after months alone in a prison camp cell, none of this seemed real.

'Tell me,' said the Dodger to the officer, 'what is all this about?'

'You will find out soon,' said the officer. 'Now change into your new clothes. You will feel much more comfortable.'

'Look here, I'm an officer,' the Dodger said. 'Will you give me your word, as an officer, that I can wear these clothes without putting myself in a difficult position?'

'Yes', said the German at once, 'you can.'

A few hours later a thick-set man in civilian clothes came to the flat. He was very friendly to the Dodger. This man was Dr Thost: from 1938 to 1939 he had worked in London as a correspondent for a German newspaper. Now he was a fairly high official in the German Foreign Office.

He put the Dodger in a car and drove him off to the best hotel in Berlin. The Dodger blinked at the sparkling lights in the hall – it was one of the few parts of the hotel which had not been bombed.

'Will you please tell me what all this is about?' he asked Dr Thost.

'You will know soon,' said Thost. He took him up to a private room. There he introduced him to a large, fat man with a loud voice and a big smile.

'This is Dr Schmidt,' said Thost. 'Dr Schmidt is Herr Hitler's interpreter.'

'Have a drink, my dear fellow,' said Dr Schmidt. He gave the Dodger a glass of Scotch. 'Not much left of it, I'm afraid,' he said.

The Dodger looked at Dr Schmidt. It was the kind of look in a small boy's eyes when he meets Father Christmas for the first time: he doesn't know what to expect.

'You are going home, my dear sir,' said Dr Schmidt with his big smile. 'No doubt you will be seeing Mr Winston Churchill when you get to England.' Then he said, more quietly, 'The British must not ask Germany for unconditional surrender.'

And the Dodger at last understood. Germany was losing the war – there was no doubt any more about that. And Dr Schmidt was asking him to act as a go-between between the British and the German governments.

A few days later, Dr Thost drove him to Dresden, and gave him his own room in a hotel there. He was taken to meet the chief of police for lunch. The chief spoke in a friendly way about the old bond between the Germans and the British.

Everyone the Dodger met spoke in the same way. To hear them talk, it was as if the Germans could not put even a dog in a prison cell; as if they could not shoot 50 British bunny rabbits, let alone British officers.

Dr Thost took the Dodger to see the circus one night, and while they were there the sirens went. The first of the three big air-raids on Dresden had started.

When they got back to their hotel, they found it in ruins. Dr Thost took the Dodger on a bus to Weimar, which was also bombed, but they stayed there for several days. The Dodger thought about escaping again, but he didn't see it would do any good. On the other hand, staying with Thost, seeing the country and the people, and getting back to England with Schmidt's message, might possibly be useful.

At last they set off south-east. In a small town on the way to Bayreuth, someone heard them talking in English in a café. The police arrived, put them both in handcuffs and arrested them as spies.

Thost was so angry he could hardly speak. But when he found his voice the police took no notice of his protests. They were thrown into a cell, and spent two days waiting to be shot.

At night they could hear the American guns. The Dodger, who had been so patient since 1940, now felt only bitterness. Freedom was just at his fingertips, yet he was about to be shot by petty officials. And all this when the German Foreign Office itself was bowing to him as a go-between.

Thost was sweating with fright and fury, and the Dodger could not help smiling about that. But after two days the local Gestapo set them free; a message had come from Berlin, saying who they were.

Thost and the Dodger went on to Munich, and then further south and on 25 April they got to Lake Constance, on the Swiss border. That night the Dodger got away from Thost and walked up to the Swiss police.

In a couple of days he was having lunch in Berne, in Switzerland, with Army intelligence officers, and within a week the RAF flew him back to England.

It was two days before VE Day that the Dodger had dinner with Winston Churchill and the American Ambassador, and told them of his adventures.

When he got to the part about Schmidt, and no unconditional surrender, Churchill took his cigar out of his mouth and grinned from ear to ear.

41 Freedom

In February, Wings Day, Dowse, James and Jack Churchill were taken from their cells in Sachsenhausen. They were unchained and taken by train to Flossenberg concentration camp, in the Harz Mountains.

When they got there they heard the guns of execution squads, and saw bodies being carried past. They waited tensely for their own turn. But no one came for them.

After two weeks, Wings and the other prisoners could hear the sound of American guns coming closer, but just as freedom began to seem possible, the Germans took them out of the camp.

The prisoners were loaded into lorries, and driven to Dachau. This was one of the worst concentration camps in the whole of Germany. They were locked in the hut that had been the camp brothel. Again they heard the guns of the execution squads, and again they waited for their turn.

Then they heard the American guns once more – and again they were taken out of the camp and up to another one in the hills near Innsbruck. The strain of hope one minute and fear the next was pulling their nerves to pieces.

After two weeks the Germans took them across the Brenner Pass to a village in Italy. With them were 50 more important prisoners. It became clear that they were being used as hostages.

Wings Day managed to get away from the group. He met an Austrian and got him to drive him to Bolzano. There he contacted the Italian Resistance and went by car and on foot to the Allied lines.

He joined in the fighting in one town, and took over the Gestapo headquarters in another. He got another car, and drove at full speed through the German lines.

With a bursting feeling of happiness he reached an American patrol. It was Wings Day's ninth escape since being shot down in 1939, and at last he had made it. It was one day before the Italian Armistice.

It was from Wings Day that the Allies learned about the group of important prisoners up by the border. The Americans rushed a party of troops up there, and rescued them just in time. The Germans had had orders to shoot the lot.

And in the meantime, what had been happening in north compound, back in Sagan?

By July 1944 'George' was creeping out under the theatre towards the wire. 'George' was the new tunnel, and Crump and Canton had cut a trapdoor for it under a seat in the twelfth row of the theatre. They were getting rid of sand under the floor again.

There was a new 'X Organisation', but there weren't any definite plans for mass escapes. They wanted to finish 'George' and then see what the situation was. By the time the snow came, and put an end to any escape plans for the winter, 'George' had got just beyond the wire.

In the middle of January, the Russians started their winter attack, and the East Front moved towards Sagan like a whirlwind. The prisoners prayed that they would overrun the camp.

They did, but the prisoners weren't there any more. The Germans had marched them out on 26 January into 30 centimetres of snow and forced them to march a hundred kilometres, for days and nights, to Spemberg. There, they loaded them into cattle trucks.

It was a terrible trip. The prisoners had been on half-issue of food parcels for months, and they were only given one meal of barley soup on the way.

The prisoners spent two days in the cattle trucks. There was just room to sit, but not to move. The Germans let them out of the trucks near Bremen and marched them to an old condemned camp. They waited outside in the rain for seven hours, being searched, before they were let into the camp.

A lot of the men collapsed at that point. About 75 were already missing — about half of those were left behind on the way because they were ill, and the rest were just 'missing' — maybe escaped, maybe shot. Of the rest, standing there in the rain, most were ill and everyone had lost a lot of weight. They looked very bony.

The Allies crossed the Rhine and came surging up towards the prisoners but the Germans marched them straight out again, up north. A few men were shot by trigger-happy guards, and a few more were killed by guns from German planes.

The prisoners didn't know it at the time, but the guards had orders to shoot them all if they didn't reach the River Elbe by a certain day. They didn't get to the Elbe that day, but by this time the guards were getting rather careful about mass murders. They took no notice of the order.

The prisoners were sheltering in barns one day when they heard gunfire as the British 1st Army crossed the Elbe. Two days later, on 2 May, they heard firing down the road, and two tanks rumbled through the trees from the south.

The prisoners didn't know if they were German or British tanks. Then the hatch in the front tank opened, and two British soldiers stuck their heads out. The men ran up to them, screaming at the tops of their voices.

Afterwards

"It was cold-blooded murder, and we are going to track the foul criminals down."

Anthony Eden
House of Commons, May 1944

In August 1945 Wing Commander Bowes, of the RAF Special Investigation Branch, flew to Germany to find out exactly how the missing 50 had died.

There was no final proof that they had been murdered, though there wasn't much doubt about it. Bowes's job was to find out the truth and, if it was murder, to arrest the murderers.

He was a good man for the job, an ex-Special Investigation detective, with a square, red face, known for his toughness. He didn't have much to work on: prisoners' stories, the bare German reports of the deaths, and the urns of ashes with the place where the bodies were burned marked on them.

In Hamburg, he formed six interrogation teams of four men each.

The job took Bowes and his men almost two years. They searched in every camp (now full of German prisoners), and questioned 250,000 German prisoners, until at last they found clues.

By 1947 Bowes knew definitely that 46 of the 50 had been murdered in cold blood, by eighteen different Gestapo officers. Under interrogation the murderers finally confessed that they had shot the prisoners in their command in the back – in small groups, at different times, and on different empty roads.

The trial of the eighteen Gestapo men began on 1 July

1947. It was heard in No. 1 War Crimes Court in Hamburg. For 50 days – one for each dead man – the evidence piled up against them. On the fiftieth day the court found them all guilty. Five were given long prison sentences. Thirteen were condemned to death. They were hanged in Hamelin Gaol, near Hamburg, on 28 February, 1948.

Bowes still did not know exactly how the other four men had died: Tim Walenn; Picard, a Belgian; Gordon Brettell; Marcinkus, the Lithnanian. All he knew was that they had been heading for Danzig when they escaped.

He and his men interrogated the 60 Danzig Gestapo men, now in a camp near Danzig. He found out that the man he needed was called Burchhardt.

Burchhardt, he was told, had been the top executioner at Danzig prison camp. He was an enormous, cruel man, who enjoyed whipping his victims to death.

Bowes was given the address in Danzig where Burchhardt was now living. There he met Burchhardt's wife. Her husband, she said, had run off with another woman. He had changed his name to Brandt and was working as a carpenter in a town called Kempten, near the Swiss border. She gave Bowes the address.

Bowes and his team drove all day, and got to Kempten at midnight. At one o'clock in the morning they raided the flat. Burchhardt was not there, but Toni, his mistress, was. They forced her to give the address where Burchhardt was staying.

Leaving a guard with Toni, so that she could not send a warning, Bowes posted twenty men round the block of flats where Burchhardt was living. He got the key to Burchhardt's flat from the caretaker, and at 3 a.m. he and Lyon, one of his men, softly let themselves into the flat.

It was very dark, and they felt their way to the bedroom. They stood with their pistols ready, over a dark figure asleep in bed. Then Bowes flicked on the light.

Burchhardt was awake in a second, and jumped half-way up the wall with shock. They found a loaded gun under his pillow. Burchhardt was so huge that they could not fit the handcuffs over his wrists.

Bowes checked Burchhardt's story with the stories of the Danzig Gestapo men in the camp. He found out that Burchhardt and a murder squad had driven the four captured officers to a wood about twelve kilometres from Danzig. Among the trees, twenty yards from the road, they machine-gunned them. The four died at once.

Burchhardt was brought to trial on 11 October, 1948. As before, the trial was held in the War Crimes Court in Hamburg. It lasted twenty days. Burchhardt was found guilty and condemned to death.

But later, that sentence was changed. It was four years since the murders: the authorities decided it was too long ago for them to hang Burchhardt now. Instead, he was simply given life-imprisonment.